〔美〕H. P. 洛夫克拉夫特————————著

刘华清—————————译

诗集

来自犹格斯的真菌

汉英对照

重庆大学出版社

目录

致已故的约翰·H. 富勒先生
To the Late John H. Fowler, Esq.

超自然诗歌的创作之人

Author of Poems of the Supernatural

发表于《苏格兰人》1916 年三月刊。约翰·H. 富勒是一位任职于美国联合业余刊物协会的诗人，死于不明疾病。洛夫克拉夫特曾评价："J. H. 富勒的诗歌《鬼影之森》以其可怖的幻想接近了爱伦·坡的水准。当我们考虑到它塑造出的绝妙氛围、字里行间怪异的和谐、恰到好处的头韵的使用，以及对于'惊散群鸟'这种具有绝佳画面感、能反映出树林茂密的形容词的选取，其含混的格律当然可以被原谅。富勒先生值得因其诗才和奇绝的想象被赞赏。"

Farewell, skill'd Fowler, whose weird numbers glow'd
With native genius by the Gods bestow'd;
Whose moving pen th' unbody'd shades inspir'd,
Whilst we, too crude to imitate, admir'd.
Thou haunting poet of the haunted wood,
How rapt have we o'er thy bright pages stood!
How oft with thee to heights supernal soar'd,
Or by thy aid uncanny depths explor'd!
Thine were the secrets of the gloomy glen,
Where wraiths, wind-wafted, kept their distant den;
Where sighing, spirits move the listless leaves,
And owlets nest on ruin'd castles eaves:
Forgotten fancies fill'd thy fairy field,
Nor would thy spell, save with thy body, yield!
Thy lustrous line with soul spontaneous grew,
Nor labour'd art nor pedants polish knew:
For measur'd cadence throbb'd the tuneful tide,

别了，大师富勒，你奇妙的韵律迸发

显示出诸神所赐予的天生才华；

你笔耕不辍地创作出无形的影像，

而我们，愚鲁得无法仿效，有目共赏。

你这位闹鬼树林中鬼气森森的诗人，

我们多么入迷地在你璀璨的书页停顿！

又多么频繁地随你翱翔在神圣的高处

或在你的帮助下探寻不可思议的深谷！

你掌握着黯淡无光的溪涧中的秘密，

那里的鬼灵，随风飘荡，守卫遥远的幽居；

那里叹息的灵魂吹动无精打采的叶片，

而猫头鹰筑巢于荒弃城堡的屋檐：

你童话般的田野充满被遗忘的幻影，

而你的魔咒，与身体同在，不会驯从！

你光辉的诗句生长于内心的本真，

看不到劳神的技法或迂腐的苦吟：

那整饬的韵律跳动如悦耳的潮水，

And what we shape, to thee the Muse supply'd.

With what high fortitude did thy refrain

Deny the burden of thy earthly pain!

The afflicted flesh, by force of courage borne,

Remain'd for others, but not for thee, to mourn.

Tho' now thy eyes are clos'd in ceaseless rest,

Thy mem'ry by thy living work is blest;

Life's ills are vanish'd, but thy honour'd name

Lingers in state, and knows a grateful fame:

Th eternal bard, whom changing ages scan,

Defies destruction, and survives the man.

So live, sweet spirit, to awake the heart,

And with thy song responding bliss impart:

Sing as of yore, with tuneful notes that shew

The grace of Waller [1], and the depth of Poe [2].

Scarce death is thine, whose soul but sought that land

Of fair enchantment painted by thy hand!

---

1. Waller: 指埃德蒙·沃勒（1606—1687），英国政治家、抒情诗人，以优美流畅的用韵著称。

2. Poe: 指埃德加·爱伦·坡（1809—1849），美国文豪，以哥特式的笔法开创了黑暗浪漫主义的先河。

我们需要塑造，缪斯直接向你恩馈。

你带着何等的坚韧不屈才强自按捺

抵抗尘世间痛苦为你带来的重压！

伤痛累累的肉体，被勇气的力量承担，

留给其他人，而非你自己，深深悼念。

虽然你在无尽的安眠中闭上了双眸，

你生机勃勃的作品记忆却被保佑；

生活的不堪消散，而你的美名

庄严地留存，得享感激的称颂：

永生的诗人，审视着变迁的时代，

与毁灭对抗，并使人得以存在。

生存吧，甜美的灵魂，将心灵唤起，

并用你的歌将和声的极乐传递：

歌唱如故，用悦耳的音符显露

沃勒的优雅，以及坡的深度。

你并未死去，只是灵魂将乐土追随

那里美丽的沉醉被你亲手描绘！

未知
The Unknown

　　出自洛夫克拉夫特在 1923 年 7 月写给克拉克·阿什顿·史密斯的一封信。作者在信中谎称此诗为他人所作："……另一首用心险恶的诗歌是伊丽莎白·伯克利的《未知》，伯克利小姐的风格相比乔丹小姐更加奔放，并描绘出在业余写作中相当少见的、充满荒凉阴晦的恐怖图景。虽然难以评判如此怪异的一首作品的真正价值，但我们姑且认为对于斜体字和加粗字体的使用是不可取的。作者应该将一切着重强调的部分通过言语表达，而非通过打印设备。"

A seething sky—
    A mottled moon—
Waves surging high—
    Storm's raving rune;

Wild clouds a-reel—
    Wild winds a-shout—
Black vapours steal
    In ghastly rout.

Thro' rift is shot
    The moon's wan grace—
But God! That blot
    Upon its face!

天空正在涌动——

　　月亮布满瘢痕——

海浪高高翻腾——

　　风暴勾画符文；

乱云不停旋转——

　　狂风不断呼啸——

黑色迷雾趁暗

　　妖鬼一般溃逃。

裂缝浅浅映入

　　月亮素雅的光——

神啊！一团污物

　　挂满她的脸庞！

坡仙的梦魇
The Poe-et's Nightmare

诗歌的核心段落"可怕的真理"发表于《漂泊者》1918年七月刊。主标题意为"爱伦·坡式的诗人所做的噩梦",此外借用另一位文豪苏轼的雅号"坡仙",译为坡仙的梦魇。

A Fable

Luxus tumultus semper causa est.

Lucullus Languish [1], student of the skies,
And connoisseur of rarebits and mince pies,
A bard by choice, a grocer's clerk by trade,
(Grown pessimist thro' honours long delay'd),
A secret yearning bore, that he might shine
In breathing numbers, and in song divine.
Each day his fountain pen was wont to drop
An ode or dirge or two about the shop,
Yet naught could strike the chord within his heart
That throbb'd for poesy, and cry'd for art.

---

1. Lucullus Languish：这个姓名由另两个姓名拼凑而成，其中名字来自罗马将军卢修斯·李锡尼·卢库勒斯，姓氏则来自英国戏剧大师谢里丹《情敌》中的角色莉迪亚·兰格维施。

寓言

穷奢极欲乃万恶之源。

卢库勒斯·兰格维施，诸天的学究，
以及干酪和百果派的鉴赏能手，
以诗人为生，以食杂店员为职，
（由于迟来的荣誉成为悲观人士），
暗中渴望的话痨，他或会炫技
轻声唱出韵律，与神圣的歌曲。
每一天他的自来水笔都习惯洒落
一两首关于商店的颂诗或挽歌，
而哪首都不能打动他的内心之弦
它为诗意而颤抖，并哀求美感。

Each eve he sought his bashful Muse to wake

With overdoses of ice-cream and cake;

But tho' th' ambitious youth a dreamer grew,

Th' Aonian[1] Nymph[2] declin'd to come to view.

Sometimes at dusk he scour'd the heav'ns afar,

Searching for raptures in the evening star;

One night he strove to catch a tale untold

In crystal deeps—but only caught a cold.

So pin'd Lucullus with his lofty woe,

Till one drear day he bought a set of Poe:

Charm'd with the cheerful horrors there display'd,

He vow'd with gloom to woo the Heav'nly Maid.

Of Auber's[3] tarn and Yaanek's[4] slope he dreams,

And weaves an hundred Ravens[5] in his schemes.

Not far from our young hero's peaceful home

Lies the fair grove wherein he loves to roam.

Tho' but a stunted copse in vacant lot,

---

1. Aonian: 爱奥尼亚，古希腊艺术风格，以纤细秀美为特征。

2. Nymph: 宁芙，希腊神话中出没于山林水泽之间的仙女。

3. Auber: 奥伯湖，爱伦·坡诗歌《尤娜路姆》中的虚构地点。

4. Yaanek: 耶涅山，爱伦·坡诗歌《尤娜路姆》中的虚构地点。洛夫克拉夫特在小说《疯狂山脉》中引用了《尤娜路姆》中与此地名相关的选段。

5. Raven: 爱伦·坡最广为人知的诗歌之一便是《乌鸦》。

每个傍晚为将害羞的缪斯唤醒

他都吃下过量的冰激凌和糕饼；

虽然有志青年逐渐成为梦想家，

爱奥尼亚的宁芙却人间蒸发。

有时他会在薄暮将远空寻觅，

搜索黄昏之星所带来的狂喜；

一晚他竭力将未知的歌谣寻找

于晶莹的深渊——却只患上了感冒。

憔悴的卢库勒斯满怀崇高的痛苦，

直到沉闷的一天他买到坡的丛书：

为书中呈现的动人恐惧着迷，

他忧郁地立誓追求天仙般的少女。

将奥伯湖与耶涅山的坡地幻想，

并将一百只乌鸦编入他的提纲。

在我们年轻的主人公宁静的家园附近

有他喜爱在此徘徊的美丽树林。

虽然空地上只有发育不良的矮树，

He dubs it Tempe [1], and adores the spot;

When shallow puddles dot the wooded plain,

And brim o'er muddy banks with muddy rain,

He calls them limpid lakes or poison pools

(Depending on which bard his fancy rules).

'Tis here he comes with Heliconian [2] fire

On Sundays when he smites the Attic lyre;

And here one afternoon he brought his gloom,

Resolv'd to chant a poet's lay of doom.

Roget's Thesaurus [3], and a book of rhymes,

Provide the rungs whereon his spirit climbs:

With this grave retinue he trod the grove

And pray'd the Fauns he might a Poe-et prove.

But sad to tell, ere Pegasus flew high,

The not unrelish'd supper hour drew nigh;

Our tuneful swain th' imperious call attends,

And soon above the groaning table bends.

---

1. Tempe: 坦佩，古希腊地名，月桂丛生、流水潺潺的美丽峡谷，被誉为"阿波罗和缪斯喜爱的去处"。

2. Helicon: 赫利孔山，位于希腊维奥蒂亚州赫利孔山脉，相传为掌管艺术与青春的缪斯女神们居住之处，象征着灵感与艺术的源泉。

3. Roget's Thesaurus: 罗格特同义词词典，面向英语使用者的著名辞书，由英国医生、自然神学家彼得·马克·罗格特在1805年编纂，多次再版后已收录了超过20000个英语词汇的同义词列表。

他将此处誉为坦佩，并极尽爱慕；

当浅浅的积水布满多树的平原，

而浑浊的雨水充溢泥泞的浅滩，

他将其称作清澈之湖或剧毒之池

（取决于哪位诗人将他的幻想统治）。

他怀着赫利孔式的激情来到此地

在星期天将雅典式的诗琴敲击；

而某一天下午他带来了他的忧愁，

决心把一位诗人多灾的歌谣吟奏。

罗格特同义词词典，以及一本韵书，

提供了阶梯供他的灵魂踏足：

他与这庄严的随从一同漫步在树林

并祈求半神自己成为坡仙般的诗人。

但悲伤的是，在天马行空之前，

便迎来了并非无趣的晚餐时间；

我们吟咏的青年感到急切的号召，

很快便向着满满当当的餐桌弯腰。

Tho' it were too prosaic to relate

Th' exact particulars of what he ate

(Such long-drawn lists the hasty reader skips,

Like Homer's well-known catalogue of ships [1]),

This much we swear: that as adjournment near'd,

A monstrous lot of cake had disappear'd!

Soon to his chamber the young bard repairs,

And courts soft Somnus [2] with sweet Lydian [3] airs;

Thro' open casement scans the star-strown deep,

And 'neath Orion's beams sinks off to sleep.

Now start from airy dell the elfin train

That dance each midnight o'er the sleeping plain,

To bless the just, or cast a warning spell

On those who dine not wisely, but too well.[4]

First Deacon Smith they plague, whose nasal glow

---

1. Catalogue of Ships: 船名表，荷马史诗《伊利亚特》第二卷中的清单。荷马在清单中列出了前往特洛伊的希腊联军中每个领导人的姓名、各自王国的定居点、各自的血统，以及他们所属船队的船只数量。或言荷马的船名表是一切清单的源头。

2. Somnus: 索莫诺斯，罗马神话中的睡神。

3. Lydia: 吕底亚，小亚细亚古国，遗址位于当代土耳其的西北部，以富庶和好战著称。

4. On those who dine not wisely, but too well: 化用自莎士比亚《奥赛罗》中的诗句 "Of one that loved not wisely but too well"。

虽然太过单调以至于无须描写
他吃掉的那些东西的具体细节
（急迫的读者会将一长串清单略掉，
就像是荷马尽人皆知的船名表），
我们只说一点：随着终场的临近，
不可胜数的蛋糕已经荡然无存！
很快年轻的诗人回到了他的卧室，
并用吕底亚的香氛吸引着索莫诺斯；
透过敞开的窗扉扫视繁星密布的深空，
并在猎户座的光芒之下沉入睡梦。
此刻从空气之谷出发的精灵的行伍
每个午夜都在沉睡的平原之上起舞，
赐福于义人，或将警告的咒语施放
在那些用餐时丰盛而不智的人们身上。
它们先是缠扰狄肯·史密斯，他的鼻息

Comes from what Holmes [1] hath call'd "Elixir Pro";

Group'd round the couch his visage they deride,

Whilst thro' his dreams unnumber'd serpents glide.

Next troop the little folk into the room

Where snores our young Endymion [2] , swath'd in gloom:

A smile lights up his boyish face, whilst he

Dreams of the moon—or what he ate at tea.

The chieftain elf th' unconscious youth surveys,

And on his form a strange enchantment lays:

Those lips, that lately thrill'd with frosted cake,

Uneasy sounds in slumbrous fashion make;

At length their owner's fancies they rehearse,

And lisp this awesome Poe-em in blank verse:

Aletheia Phrikodes

Omnia risus et omnia pulvis et omnia nihil.

Demoniac clouds, up-pil'd in chasmy reach

Of soundless heav'n, smother'd the brooding night;

Nor came the wonted whisp'rings of the swamp,

---

1. Holmes: 指奥利弗·温德尔·霍姆斯（1809—1894），美国医生、诗人、博物学家。霍姆斯在诗歌《医学博士瑞普·凡·温克尔》中虚构了一种主要由酒精构成的"灵丹妙药"。

2. Endymion: 恩底弥翁，希腊神话中在长眠中永葆青春的美男子。

来自被霍姆斯称为"灵丹妙药"的东西；

它们环绕着卧床嘲笑着他的面容，

而无数的长蛇爬动着穿过他的梦境。

随后小仙子们结队进入另一间屋

我们年轻的恩底弥翁在打鼾，被黑暗束缚：

笑容点亮他孩子气的脸庞，当他

梦到了月亮——或大饱口福地用茶。

精灵的首领将沉睡的青年注目，

并在他的身上降下了奇异的咒术：

不久前为糖霜蛋糕发颤的嘴唇，

在昏昏沉沉中发出不安的声音；

最后它们复述了自己主人的幻想，

将可怕的坡式诗歌道于黑暗的诗行：

可怕的真理

一切皆欢笑，一切皆尘土，一切皆虚无。

恶魔般的云朵，堆积的裂隙区域

位于寂静的高空，窒息了忧思的黑夜；

没有寻常的低语从沼泽传来，

Nor voice of autumn wind along the moor,

Nor mutter'd noises of th' insomnious grove

Whose black recesses never saw the sun.

Within that grove a hideous hollow lies,

Half bare of trees; a pool in centre lurks

That none dares sound; a tarn of murky face

(Tho' naught can prove its hue, since light of day,

Affrighted, shuns the forest-shadow'd banks).

Hard by, a yawning hillside grotto breathes,

From deeps unvisited, a dull, dank air

That sears the leaves on certain stunted trees

Which stand about, clawing the spectral gloom

With evil boughs. To this accursed dell

Come woodland creatures, seldom to depart:

Once I behold, upon a crumbling stone

Set altar-like before the cave, a thing

I saw not clearly, yet from glimpsing, fled.

In this half-dusk I meditate alone

At many a weary noontide, when without

A world forgets me in its sun-blest mirth.

Here howl by night the werewolves, and the souls

没有秋日的声音缭绕着荒原，

没有低声的噪音传出失眠的树丛

那里幽暗的深处从未见过旭日。

在树林里面有一块可怖的洼地

几乎没有树木；当中潜伏的水池

无人敢于测量；这片湖面目不明

（无法证实它的色调，因为白昼之光，

也胆战心惊，躲开树林荫翳下的湖岸）。

附近，呼吸着一座敞开的山间岩穴，

从无人造访的深渊，沉闷潮湿的气流

枯萎了那些发育不良的树上的叶片

它们静静伫立，将幽灵般忧郁撕开的

是它们邪恶的枝条。这诅咒的山谷中

涌入了林间的生物，永远不会离去：

我曾经看到，一块破碎的岩石

像祭坛一般伫立在洞穴之前，某物

不等我看清楚，便从视线中，逃走。

在这临近薄暮之时我独自冥想

而无休的疲惫达到极致，不会有

世界将我在阳光抚慰的欢乐中遗忘。

此地的夜晚有狼人嚎叫，而那些死灵

Of those that knew me well in other days.

Yet on this night the grove spake not to me;

Nor spake the swamp, nor wind along the moor,

Nor moan'd the wind about the lonely eaves

Of the bleak, haunted pile wherein I lay.

I was afraid to sleep, or quench the spark

Of the low-burning taper by my couch.

I was afraid when thro' the vaulted space

Of the old tow'r, the clock-ticks died away

Into a silence so profound and chill

That my teeth chatter'd—giving yet no sound.

Then flicker'd low the light, and all dissolv'd,

Leaving me floating in the hellish grasp

Of body'd blackness, from whose beating wings

Came ghoulish blasts of charnel-scented mist.

Things vague, unseen, unfashion'd, and unnam'd

Jostled each other in the seething void

That gap'd, chaotic, downward to a sea

Of speechless horror, foul with writhing thoughts.

All this I felt, and felt the mocking eyes

Of the curs'd universe upon my soul;

坡仙的梦魇

本是往日与我倾心相知的人们。

而这个夜里树林没有向我发声；

沼泽没有低语，荒原未被缭绕，

孤单的屋檐间，夜风未将呜咽

传入我那凄冷诡谲的栖身之地。

我不敢睡去，或是将火花扑灭，

捻熄在卧榻旁微微燃烧的蜡烛。

我害怕自那拱形的空间之上

古老的高塔，时钟的滴答消散

只剩下深沉冰冷的一片沉默

我牙齿打颤——却没有发出声响。

随后光芒低低摇曳，一切都已消融，

留下我飘飞于那地狱般的统治

那是群成形的黑暗，拍动的翅膀下

阴森尸臭的气息如雾弥漫。

模糊、隐匿、无形、未名的影迹

彼此推搡着置身于沸腾的虚空

裂开、混沌，俯接的那处海面

有着不可名状的恐怖，被扭曲的思想玷污。

我感受到这一切，以及嘲弄的眼眸

来自被诅咒的宇宙，加诸我的心灵；

Yet naught I saw nor heard, till flash'd a beam

Of lurid lustre thro' the rotting heav'ns,

Playing on scenes I labour'd not to see.

Methought the nameless tarn, alight at last,

Reflected shapes, and more reveal'd within

Those shocking depths than ne'er were seen before;

Methought from out the cave a demon train,

Grinning and smirking, reel'd in fiendish rout;

Bearing within their reeking paws a load

Of carrion viands for an impious feast.

Methought the stunted trees with hungry arms

Grop'd greedily for things I dare not name;

The while a stifling, wraith-like noisomeness

Fill'd all the dale, and spoke a larger life

Of uncorporeal hideousness awake

In the half-sentient wholeness of the spot.

Now glow'd the ground, and tarn, and cave, and trees,

And moving forms, and things not spoken of,

With such a phosphorescence as men glimpse

In the putrescent thickets of the swamp

Where logs decaying lie, and rankness reigns.

但我没有见闻，直到射下的光芒

穿越衰败的天国带来骇人的光彩，

掠过那些我竭力不想看到的景致。

我看到无名的湖泊，最终被照耀，

反射出阴影，而水中愈加露出

那些从未被如此直视的可怖深渊；

我看到洞穴外有一支恶魔的队列，

露齿冷笑，幸灾乐祸，溃败间四处逃窜；

它们恶臭的利爪之中紧握着许多

为亵渎的盛筵所准备的珍馐腐肉。

我看到低矮的树丛伸出饥渴的手臂

贪婪地搜寻着那些我不敢命名之物；

同时令人窒息的幽魂般的剧臭

充斥整座山谷，表明某个巨型存在

满怀着捉摸不定的恐怖并觉醒

在此地半梦半醒的整体之内。

此刻亮起的地面、湖泊、洞穴、树林，

移动的影迹，和未曾提及的种种，

连成了一片磷光使得人们瞥见

在沼泽即将腐烂的繁茂之处

横置着衰朽的原木，并被腐臭统辖。

Methought a fire-mist drap'd with lucent fold

The well-remember'd features of the grove,

Whilst whirling ether bore in eddying streams

The hot, unfinish'd stuff of nascent worlds

Hither and thither thro' infinities

Of light and darkness, strangely intermix'd;

Wherein all entity had consciousness,

Without th' accustom'd outward shape of life.

Of these swift-circling currents was my soul,

Free from the flesh, a true constituent part;

Nor felt I less myself, for want of form.

Then clear'd the mist, and o'er a star-strown scene,

Divine and measureless, I gaz'd in awe.

Alone in space, I view'd a feeble fleck

Of silvern light, marking the narrow ken

Which mortals call the boundless universe.

On ev'ry side, each as a tiny star,

Shone more creations, vaster than our own,

And teeming with unnumber'd forms of life;

Tho' we as life would recognise it not,

Being bound to earthy thoughts of human mould.

坡仙的梦魇

我看到火色迷雾以透明的褶皱覆盖

树林当中那些难以忘怀的身影，

而以太的漩涡凿入湍急的溪流

新生世界中炽热而未完成的事物

无处不在地越过无穷无尽的

光明与暗影，诡异地交织混杂；

在那里一切的实体都具有知觉，

却没有通常而言生命拥有的外形。

这些飞速旋转的激流间是我的灵魂，

超脱于肉体，真正的核心要素；

我并未感觉自身缺失，要把形体索求。

随后迷雾散去，下方星光熠熠的景象，

神圣又不可测量，我敬畏地注目。

独处于太虚，我看到微弱的一小片

银色光芒，标出的狭窄的领域

被凡人们称为广袤无垠的宇宙。

每个方向上，每一粒渺小的恒星，

都照亮更多的造物，远比我们壮阔，

并充满了不可胜数的生命的形态；

虽然我们无法将它们作为生命认出，

受限于人类的天性中尘俗的念头。

As on a moonless night the Milky Way

In solid sheen displays its countless orbs

To weak terrestrial eyes, each orb a sun;

So beam'd the prospect on my wond'ring soul:

A spangled curtain, rich with twinkling gems,

Yet each a mighty universe of suns.

But as I gaz'd, I sens'd a spirit voice

In speech didactic, tho' no voice it was,

Save as it carried thought. It bade me mark

That all the universes in my view

Form'd but an atom in infinity;

Whose reaches pass the ether-laden realms

Of heat and light, extending to far fields

Where flourish worlds invisible and vague,

Fill'd with strange wisdom and uncanny life,

And yet beyond; to myriad spheres of light,

To spheres of darkness, to abysmal voids

That know the pulses of disorder'd force.

Big with these musings, I survey'd the surge

Of boundless being, yet I us'd not eyes,

For spirit leans not on the props of sense.

在这个无月的夜里的璀璨星河

以繁密的光辉展现不计其数的星体

在尘世间虚弱的眼前，每颗都如同太阳；

这一幕景象如是照映着我惊诧的心灵：

一条晶莹的帘幕，布满闪耀的宝石，

每一个宏伟的寰宇都由繁星组构。

但在我凝视之时，我感到有灵体发出

说教般的话语，虽然并没有声音，

只有它送来的思绪。它吩咐我铭记

在我视线当中的诸天世界不过

如同一个原子在兆载永劫中成形；

它们的领地跨过充满以太的区域

之中的光与热量，延伸至遥远的处所

那里大批滋生的世界无形而模糊，

充满奇异的智慧与不可思议的生命，

在此之外；有着无数光明的星球，

有着黑暗的群星，有着虚空的深渊

深深知晓着混沌之力的脉动。

满载着这些沉思，我详细探查着

无限的存在的洪流，却没有使用双眸，

因为精神并不依托于感官的支柱。

The docent presence swell'd my strength of soul;
All things I knew, but knew with mind alone.
Time's endless vista spread before my thought
With its vast pageant of unceasing change
And sempiternal strife of force and will;
I saw the ages flow in stately stream
Past rise and fall of universe and life;
I saw the birth of suns and worlds, their death,
Their transmutation into limpid flame,
Their second birth and second death, their course
Perpetual thro' the aeons' termless flight,
Never the same, yet born again to serve
The varying purpose of omnipotence.
And whilst I watch'd, I knew each second's space
Was greater than the lifetime of our world.
Then turn'd my musings to that speck of dust
Whereon my form corporeal took its rise;
That speck, born but a second, which must die
In one brief second more; that fragile earth;
That crude experiment; that cosmic sport
Which holds our proud, aspiring race of mites

这讲解的灵体激发了我灵魂的力量;

我知晓了一切,又仅是知晓于心。

时间无尽的幻象在我思绪前展开

呈现出瞬息万变的宏伟的盛装游行

以及力量与心智之间永恒的争斗;

我看到岁月在浩瀚的河流中逝去

穿越了宇宙与生命的兴衰沉浮;

我看到恒星与世界的诞生,它们的毁灭,

它们蜕变为透明的烈焰的过程,

它们再次的诞生与毁灭,它们的旅途

永无休止地穿过万古无尽的飞翔,

常变常新,却再一次降生以服从

全知全能者变幻莫测的意图。

在我观望之时,我知道每一秒的范畴

都远大于我们的世界拥有的生命周期。

随后我将沉思转向了一点尘埃

我有形的肉体在那里得以产生;

那个小点,诞生仅仅一秒,必然死去

于再过一秒之后;那脆弱的地球;

是残酷的实验,或宇宙的玩耍

将我们蜉蝣般骄傲自大的种族束缚

And moral vermin; those presuming mites

Whom ignorance with empty pomp adorns,

And misinstructs in specious dignity;

Those mites who, reas'ning outward, vaunt themselves

As the chief work of Nature, and enjoy

In fatuous fancy the particular care

Of all her mystic, super-regnant pow'r.

And as I strove to vision the sad sphere

Which lurk'd, lost in ethereal vortices,

Methought my soul, tun'd to the infinite,

Refus'd to glimpse that poor atomic blight;

That misbegotten accident of space;

That globe of insignificance, whereon

(My guide celestial told me) dwells no part

Of empyrean virtue, but where breed

The coarse corruptions of divine disease;

The fest'ring ailments of infinity;

The morbid matter by itself call'd man:

Such matter (said my guide) as oft breaks forth

On broad Creation's fabric, to annoy

For a brief instant, ere assuaging death

如心灵的害虫；这些恣肆的蜉蝣

其懵懂无知被空幻的盛景装扮，

并以徒有其表的自尊倒行逆施；

这些蜉蝣们，表面理性，吹嘘自己为

大自然最杰出的作品，所享受的

愚昧的幻影中专属的特殊看护

来自她神秘的支配全局的力量。

当我竭力想看清那颗悲伤的星球

是如何潜伏并失落于以太的漩涡，

我看到我的灵魂，再次转向无穷，

拒绝瞥视那可怜的原子般的祸端；

那颗太空之中身份可鄙的灾殃；

那微不足道的行星，在它上面

（我的引路之灵告知）找不到一丝

天堂般的美德，但却滋生出

神圣的疫病引发的粗鄙的堕落；

那是无穷患有的化脓的顽疾；

那病态的物质将自己称为人类：

这种物质（我的向导说）惯于突然爆发

在造物广袤的格局中，只为滋扰

短暂的一瞬，直到平息一切的死亡

Heal up the malady its birth provok'd.
Sicken'd, I turn'd my heavy thoughts away.
Then spake th' ethereal guide with mocking mien,
Upbraiding me for searching after Truth;
Visiting on my mind the searing scorn
Of mind superior; laughing at the woe
Which rent the vital essence of my soul.
Methought he brought remembrance of the time
When from my fellows to the grove I stray'd,
In solitude and dusk to meditate
On things forbidden, and to pierce the veil
Of seeming good and seeming beauteousness
That covers o'er the tragedy of Truth,
Helping mankind forget his sorry lot,
And raising Hope where Truth would crush it down.
He spake, and as he ceas'd, methought the flames
Of fuming Heav'n resolv'd in torments dire;
Whirling in maelstroms of rebellious might,
Yet ever bound by laws I fathom'd not.
Cycles and epicycles, of such girth
That each a cosmos seem'd, dazzled my gaze

治愈由它的诞生所导致的病症。

怀着厌恶，我将沉重的思维转向别处。

随后那缥缈的向导以嘲弄的态度发话，

对于我旨在真理的追寻横加指责；

逗留在我脑海中的灼人的轻蔑

带有精神的优越；它所嘲笑的悲哀

撕裂了我灵魂中至关重要的本真。

我看到他带来某个时刻的纪念

那时我离开同伴们向着树林游荡，

在薄暮与形单影只中仔细思考

禁忌的事物，试图揭穿那道帷幕

徒有其表的良善和徒有其表的优美

它实际上遮蔽着悲剧一般的真理，

并帮助着人类忘却极度的哀愁，

在真理无情碾过之处带来希望。

他作声，而当他停止，我看到烈火

自喷烟的天堂分解为可怖的磨难；

在力量桀骜难驯的大漩涡中转动，

却永远受制于我无法了解的律条。

循环与周转的圈环，画出的圆带

每一条都如同一个宇宙，使得我目眩

Till all a wild phantasmal glow became.
Now burst athwart the fulgent formlessness
A rift of purer sheen, a sight supernal,
Broader that all the void conceiv'd by man,
Yet narrow here. A glimpse of heav'ns beyond;
Of weird creations so remote and great
That ev'n my guide assum'd a tone of awe.
Borne on the wings of stark immensity,
A touch of rhythm celestial reach'd my soul;
Thrilling me more with horror than with joy.
Again the spirit mock'd my human pangs,
And deep revil'd me for presumptuous thoughts:
Yet changing now his mien, he bade me scan
The wid'ning rift that clave the walls of space;
He bade me search it for the ultimate;
He bade me find the Truth I sought so long;
He bade me brave th' unutterable Thing,
The final Truth of moving entity.
All this he bade and offer'd—but my soul,
Clinging to life, fled without aim or knowledge,
Shrieking in silence thro' the gibbering deeps.

直到全部汇集为一束幽灵般的光芒。

此刻在灿烂的无形中相对地爆发出

一道更加纯粹的光辉，一幕神圣的景象，

比人类所设想的一切虚空更加广阔，

却在此显得狭小。它透漏出至高的苍旻；

那些遥远而又伟大的诡秘造物

甚至使我的向导在语调中表露惊恐。

被空无一物的无限的羽翼所承载，

一丝天上的韵律将我的灵魂触及；

使我更多地由于恐惧而非快乐颤抖。

那个灵体再次嘲弄着我人类的苦楚，

并严厉地责骂着我自以为是的念头：

但此刻他神情突变，并吩咐我扫视

分开了宇宙幕墙的宽阔的裂口；

他吩咐我在里面寻找终极答案；

他吩咐我将苦苦求索的真理探寻；

他吩咐我直面那不可名状之物，

关于变化着的本质的最终真理。

他吩咐这一切并开价——我的灵魂，

依附于生命，无知又盲目地逃窜，

在充满呓语的深渊中发出无声的哀鸣。

Thus shriek'd the young Lucullus, as he fled
Thro' gibbering deeps—and tumbled out of bed;
Within the room the morning sunshine gleams,
Whilst the poor youth recalls his troubled dreams.
He feels his aching limbs, whose woeful pain
Informs his soul his body lives again,
And thanks his stars—or cosmoses—or such
That he survives the noxious nightmare's clutch.
Thrill'd with the music of th' eternal spheres
(Or is it the alarm-clock that he hears?),
He vows to all the Pantheon, high and low,
No more to feed on cake, or pie, or Poe.
And now his gloomy spirits seem to rise,
As he the world beholds with clearer eyes;
The cup he thought too full of dregs to quaff
Affords him wine enough to raise a laugh.
(All this is metaphor—you must not think
Our late Endymion prone to stronger drink!)
With brighter visage and with lighter heart,
He turns his fancies to the grocer's mart;
And strange to say, at last he seems to find

年轻的卢库勒斯如是哀鸣，并且逃出

充满呓语的深渊——而跌下了床铺；

在这被清晨的阳光照亮的房间之中，

可怜的青年回想起他不安的梦境。

他感到四肢发痛，那极度的苦涩

告知灵魂他的身体已再度存活，

感谢他的主星——或宇宙——或其他

他得以幸免于梦魇毒害无穷的利爪。

战栗于永恒的天体所发出的乐曲

（或者他听到的只是闹钟的响起？）

他向诸神中不论尊卑的每一位发誓，

再也不以蛋糕、馅饼，或坡仙为主食。

如今他阴郁的精神似乎得以缓解，

并用更加澄澈的双眼观察着世界；

他本觉得满是渣滓不愿畅饮的酒杯

提供给了他足以带来欢笑的酒水。

（这只是个隐喻——请不要想象

我们之前的恩底弥翁变成一个酒囊！）

带着明亮的脸庞和更加轻盈的心态，

他将他的爱好转向了食杂店的柜台；

说起来奇怪，到最后他似乎确认

His daily duties worthy of his mind.
Since Truth prov'd such a high and dang'rous goal,
Our bard seeks one less trying to his soul;
With deep-drawn breath he flouts his dreary woes,
And a good clerk from a bad poet grows!
Now close attend my lay, ye scribbling crew
That bay the moon in numbers strange and new;
That madly for the spark celestial bawl
In metres short or long, or none at all:
Curb your rash force, in numbers or at tea,
Nor overzealous for high fancies be;
Reflect, ere ye the draught Pierian [1] take,
What worthy clerks or plumbers ye might make;
Wax not too frenzied in the leaping line
That neither sense nor measure can confine,
Lest ye, like young Lucullus Launguish, groan
Beneath Poe-etic nightmares of your own!

---

1. Pieria: 比埃里亚，希腊中北部州名，相传这里的泉水被缪斯女神赐福，任何人只要喝下便可获得文学和艺术上的灵感。

坡仙的梦魇

他的日常工作完全值得他用心。

既然真理具有如此奢侈又危险的目的，

我们的诗人设法让他的灵魂不再奋起；

他凭借深呼吸无视了自己阴沉的哀痛，

一位优秀的职员从糟糕的诗人中诞生！

现在靠近我的位置，乱涂乱写的你们

曾向月亮嗥叫发出崭新怪异的音韵；

为了天空中的火花而疯狂地大吼

以或短或长的格律，或是一无所有：

抑制你们的冲动，在作韵或用茶时，

也不要对崇高的幻想如醉如痴；

想一想，当你们还未饮下比埃里亚的圣泉，

是否能够成为有价值的水管工或职员；

不要在起跳线上变得太过狂野

令理智或是标准没有办法制约，

以免像年轻的卢库勒斯·兰格维施一样

在你们自身的坡仙风格的梦魇中哭嚷！

辙痕下的路
The Rutted Road

发表于《试验》1917 年一月刊。

Bleak autumn mists send down their chilly load,
A raven shivers as he flutters by;
Thro' lonely pasture winds the Rutted Road
Where bord'ring elms loom bare against the sky.

Those deep-sunk tracks, which dumbly point ahead
O'er travell'd sands that stretch to Vision's rim,
Wake hidden thoughts—a longing half a dread—
Till Fancy pauses at the prospect dim.

Descending shadows bid me haste along
The ancient ruts so many knew before;
A cricket mocks me with his mirthless song—
I fear the path—I fain would see no more.

Yet here, with ox-drawn cart, each thoughtless swain
His course pursu'd, nor left the common way;
Can I, superior to the rustic train,
On brighter by-roads find the dawning day?

暗淡的秋雾将浓密的冰冷飘扬，
一只寒鸦战栗着惊飞而去；
辙痕下的路蜿蜒穿过荒凉的牧场
两旁赤裸的榆树高耸直入天际。

那些沉陷的车辙，默默向前延伸
越过抵达幻境边缘的铺路之沙，
唤醒隐秘的思绪——渴望几近于销魂——
直到空想在昏暗的征途前停下。

迫近的阴影使我独自匆匆奔行
在人尽皆知的古代辙痕上面；
一只蟋蟀用它忧郁的歌将我嘲弄
我害怕这条路——我希望永不再见。

此地，在牛车里，每个无心的村夫
都循路而行，不曾离开寻常的轨道；
而我，能否超过那支乡间的行伍，
在明亮的岔路上将破晓的清晨寻找？

With questing look I scan the dark'ning moor;
Perchance o'er yonder mound all blessings wait;
But still the Rutted Road's resistless lure
Constrains my progress to the Path of Fate.

So must I grope between the brooding trees
Where those before me found the mystic night;
I travel onward, past the wither'd leas—
But what, beyond the bend, awaits my sight?

Do fairer lands than this invite my feet?
Will Fate on me her choicest boons bestow?
What lies ahead, my weary soul to greet?
Why is it that I do not wish to know?

我用探寻的目光扫遍黑暗的沼泽；

也许所有的祝福都在那座山丘等候；

但是辙痕下的路难以抗拒的诱惑

强迫我朝着这条命运之路行走。

所以我探索在幽深的树林之内

我的前人们在此地初识神秘的夜；

我向前赶路，穿越过荒草枯萎——

但什么，在拐弯之后，会进入我的视野？

是否更美的土地呼唤着我的脚步前行？

命运能否赐予我至高无上的宠爱？

什么在前方，将会迎接我疲惫的心灵？

为什么我根本不希望自己明白？

涅墨西斯
Nemesis

发表于《漂泊者》1918年六月刊。洛夫克拉夫特曾说："这首诗表达了一种可被正统想法所接受的概念，梦魇作为一种惩罚降临于在古老的岁月中铸成大错的灵魂之上——甚至跨越了数百万年！"作者本人也在小说《夜魔》中引用了这首诗的选段。涅墨西斯是希腊神话中的复仇女神，克苏鲁神话中的外神格赫罗斯也被称为涅墨西斯之星。

Thro' the ghoul-guarded [1] gateways of slumber,

Past the wan-moon'd abysses of night,

I have liv'd o'er my lives without number,

I have sounded all things with my sight;

And I struggle and shriek ere the daybreak, being driven to

madness with fright.

I have whirl'd with the earth at the dawning,

When the sky was a vaporous flame;

I have seen the dark universe yawning,

Where the black planets roll without aim;

Where they roll in their horror unheeded, without knowledge

or lustre or name.

---

1. ghoul: 食尸鬼，克苏鲁神话中的虚构种族，一种食腐的夜行性类人生物。食尸鬼由人类变异而来，并且与人类社会关系密切。

涅墨西斯

穿越食尸鬼守卫的沉睡门户，

在白月照耀的夜之深渊彼方，

我经历过的复生已不可计数，

我用自己的视线将万物奏响；

而我在破晓前挣扎着惊叫，满怀着恐惧坠入疯狂。

我曾在黎明与地球一同萦回，

蒸腾的烈火充满彼时的天空，

我见过昏暗的宇宙张开大嘴，

漆黑的行星在此盲目地转动，

带着它们饱经忽视的恐怖，无知、无光亦无名。

I had drifted o'er seas without ending,
Under sinister grey-clouded skies
That the many-fork'd lightning is rending,
That resound with hysterical cries;
With the moans of invisible daemons that out of
　　the green waters rise.

I have plung'd like a deer thro' the arches
Of the hoary primordial grove,
Where the oaks feel the presence that marches
And stalks on where no spirit dares rove;
And I flee from a thing that surrounds me, and
　　leers thro' dead branches above.

I have stumbled by cave-ridden mountains
That rise barren and bleak from the plain,
I have drunk of the fog-foetid fountains
That ooze down to the marsh and the main;
And in hot cursed tarns I have seen things I care
　　not to gaze on again.

我曾漂荡在无穷无尽的海面，

头顶不祥的天穹被灰云遮蔽，

多岔的枝状闪电正从中裂断，

回响着阵阵歇斯底里的哭泣，

无形的恶魔将呻吟混入，它们从万顷碧涛中升起。

我曾如同小鹿一样跃入拱门，

置身于暮气沉沉的原始林木，

那里的橡树感到有灵体行进

并蹑足于幽魂不敢徘徊之处；

某物从上方的枯枝外睨视，而我从它的包围中逃出。

我曾跋涉的洞穴密布的群山

荒凉贫瘠地升起在平原之上，

我曾啜饮的恶雾染臭的泉眼

缓缓流淌着注入沼泽与海洋；

而诅咒的沸湖中所见之物，我留心不再将它凝望。

I have scann'd the vast ivy-clad palace,
I have trod its untenanted hall,
Where the moon writhing up from the valleys
Shews the tapestried things on the wall;
Strange figures discordantly woven, which I cannot
  endure to recall.

I have peer'd from the casement in wonder
At the mouldering meadows around,
At the many-roof'd village laid under
The curse of a grave-girdled ground;
And from rows of white urn-carven marble I listen
  intently for sound.

I have haunted the tombs of the ages,
I have flown on the pinions of fear
Where the smoke-belching Erebus[1] *rages,*
Where the jokulls loom snow-clad and drear:
And in realms where the sun of the desert consumes
  what it never can cheer.

---

1. Erebus: 厄瑞玻斯，希腊神话中的黑暗幽冥之神。

我曾端详过青藤覆盖的王宫

并在它空无一人的大厅盘桓，

那里的月亮自山谷翻滚上升

将绣帷般的影迹在墙上显现；

奇形异状毫不和谐地交织，我无法忍受将它追念。

我曾透过窗扉向外愕然窥视，

环绕在四周的草地渐渐腐朽，

挤满了屋顶的村镇无法自制

陷入坟墓合围的地表的诅咒。

在白色石瓮的行列当中，我专心致志将声音聆受。

我曾徘徊在岁月的坟茔之间，

我曾飞舞过那双恐惧的羽翼，

那里厄瑞玻斯愤然喷出浓烟，

那里阴郁积雪之山赫然耸立：

那片国度中的沙漠之日，将它不喜之物付之一炬。

I was old when the Pharaohs first mounted
The jewel-deck'd throne by the Nile;
I was old in those epochs uncounted
When I, and I only, was vile;
And Man, yet untainted and happy, dwelt in bliss on
*   the far Arctic isle.*

Oh, great was the sin of my spirit,
And great is the reach of its doom;
Not the pity of Heaven can cheer it,
Nor can respite be found in the tomb:
Down the infinite aeons come beating the wings of
*   unmerciful gloom.*

Thro' the ghoul-guarded gateways of slumber,
Past the wan-moon'd abysses of night,
I have liv'd o'er my lives without number,
I have sounded all things with my sight;
And I struggle and shriek ere the daybreak, being
*   driven to madness with fright.*

我老去时法老们才初次荣登

尼罗河岸边镶满宝石的王座；

我老去在数不清的纪元之中

那时我，只有我，代表邪恶；

而人类，无瑕又欢愉，身处北极的岛屿享受极乐。

啊，我的灵魂有着弥天大罪，

而它所带来的劫难影响深重；

天堂的怜悯并不能将它抚慰，

而坟墓之中它同样不得安宁：

直至于无限的万古，那无情的晦暗双翼仍会拍动。

穿越食尸鬼守卫的沉睡门户，

在白月照耀的夜之深渊彼方，

我经历过的复生已不可计数，

我用自己的视线将万物奏响；

而我在破晓前挣扎着惊叫，满怀着恐惧坠入疯狂。

星空恐惧症
Astrophobos

发表于《美国联合业余刊物协会会刊》1918年一月刊，
洛夫克拉夫特谎称此诗由他人所作："沃德·菲利普斯的作
品《星空恐惧症》是另一首拥有诀窍的诗歌，虽然这首诗歌
的诀窍更加难以理解并强烈不推荐新人效仿。评论家会将按
照这种诀窍创作出的诗歌称为'尤娜路姆'式，因为它带有
爱伦·坡的许多特征。作为典型，这首诗的尤娜路姆式体现
在华丽的血红色、骇人距离外的景象、独创的短语、不同寻
常的用词，以及或神秘主义或含混不清的总体思路。这首诗
对于那些喜爱头脑中的鱼子酱的美食家来说是一场盛宴，但
它远远满足不了克莱纳先生《露丝》一类的正常的诗歌品味。"

In the midnight heavens burning
Thro' ethereal deeps afar,
Once I watch'd with restless yearning
An alluring, aureate star;
Ev'ry eye aloft returning,
Gleaming nigh the Arctic car [1].

Mystic waves of beauty blended
With the gorgeous golden rays;
Phantasies of bliss descended
In a myrrh'd [2] *Elysian haze;*
And in lyre-born chords extended
Harmonies of Lydian lays.

---

1. Arctic car：大熊星座的别称。

2. myrrh：没药，产自波斯、阿拉伯及非洲东北地区的珍贵香料，也可作为防腐剂和止痛剂使用，其味苦辛。

在午夜之中燃烧着的高天

遥远而缥缈的深渊之后，

我曾带着无眠的渴望瞥见

一颗迷人、华美的星球；

每只眼睛都向着高空归还，

像北辰的战车一样剔透。

优美而神秘的波纹中掺杂

辉煌灿烂的金黄色光束；

极乐的奇思妙想坠落而下

陷入乐园中没药的薄雾；

诗琴奏出的旋律不断扩大

当中有吕底亚式的和睦。

There (thought I) lies scenes of pleasure,

Where the free and blessed dwell,

And each moment bears a treasure

Freighted with a lotus-spell [1],

And there floats a liquid measure

From the lute of Israfel [2].

There (I told myself) were shining

Worlds of happiness unknown,

Peace and Innocence entwining

By the Crowned Virtue's throne;

Men of light, their thoughts refining

Purer, fairer, than our own.

Thus I mus'd, when o'er the vision

Crept a red delirious change;

Hope dissolving to derision,

Beauty to distortion strange;

Hymnic chords in weird collision,

Spectral sights in endless range.

---

1. lotus: 指忘忧果，又译落拓枣，古希腊神话中的一种果实，吃后能让人忘记一切而变得快乐轻松。

2. Israfel: 以色拉费，《古兰经》中的音乐天使，在胸口长有诗琴的琴弦，爱伦·坡有同名诗作传世。

那里（我想）有着欢愉的景象，
自由快乐之人在此安居，
每一个时刻所带来的珍藏
都满载着忘忧果的咒语，
那里还有清澈的音律飘荡
从以色拉费的诗琴响起。

那里（我告诉自己）正闪烁着
充满未知的幸福的世界，
平和与天真无邪相互交错
与美德女神的宝座相邻；
光明之人，他们的思想变得
比我们自身更美好纯洁。

我如是沉思，当眼中的幻景
迎来血红而发狂的变异；
希望在溶解之后只剩嘲弄，
美丽转变为诡异的扭曲；
赞诗的和弦在离奇相抵中，
无穷无尽地幽幽地叹息。

Crimson burn'd the star of sadness
As behind the beams I peer'd;
All was woe that seem'd but gladness
Ere my gaze with truth was sear'd;
Cacodaemons, mir'd with madness,
Thro' the fever'd flick'ring leer'd.

Now I know the fiendish fable
That the golden glitter bore;
Now I shun the spangled sable
That I watch'd and lov'd before;
But the horror, set and stable,
Haunts my soul for evermore.

熊熊燃烧之下悲伤的星辰

被我从那些光束后窥伺；

一切表面的喜悦实为悲恨

自我的目光发现了真实；

陷入疯狂之中的恶鬼大军，

透过那狂热的闪光睨视。

如今我明白恶魔般的虚谬

来自那金色光芒的闪耀；

如今我避开的晶莹的黑裘

曾经被我仰望并且喜好；

但那份恐惧，固执而又恒久，

会永远将我的灵魂萦绕。

普绪科蓬波斯：有韵的传说
Psychopompos: A Tale in Rhyme

发表于《漂泊者》1919 年十月刊。普绪科蓬波斯是希腊神话中的接引冥神，有时也被视为赫尔墨斯的别称。

I am He who howls in the night;
I am He who moans in the snow;
I am He who hath never seen light;
I am He who mounts from below.

My car is the car of Death;
My wings are the wings of dread;
My breath is the north wind's breath;
My prey are the cold and the dead.

In old Auvergne [1], when schools were poor and few,
And peasants fancy'd what they scarcely knew,
When lords and gentry shunn'd their Monarch's throne
For solitary castles of their own,
There dwelt a man of rank, whose fortress stood
In the hush'd twilight of a hoary wood.
De Blois his name; his lineage high and vast,

---

1. Auvergne: 奥弗涅，法国中部大区，欧洲人口最稀少的地区之一。

是我在夜深时发出吼声；

是我在雪地中传出悲叹；

是我从不曾见到过光明；

是我从深渊里向上登攀。

我有着代表死亡的车驾；

我有着象征恐惧的翅膀；

我如同北风般呼吸吐纳；

我的猎物寒冷而又凋亡。

古老的奥弗涅，学校贫寒而稀疏，

农民们投身于知之甚少的事务，

领主与乡绅避开君王的宝位

藏身于他们自己独居的堡垒。

那里有一位豪人，他的城堡屹立

在宁静的暮光下灰白的树林里。

他名为德布洛斯；家世渊远浩瀚，

A proud memorial of an honour'd past;

But curious swains would whisper now and then

That Sieur De Blois was not as other men.

In person dark and lean, with glossy hair,

And gleaming teeth that he would often bare,

With piercing eye, and stealthy roving glance,

And tongue that clipt the soft, sweet speech of France;

The Sieur was little lov'd and seldom seen,

So close he kept within his own demesne.

The castle servants, few, discreet, and old,

Full many a tale of strangeness might have told;

But bow'd with years, they rarely left the door

Wherein their sires and grandsires serv'd before.

Thus gossip rose, as gossip rises best,

When mystery imparts a keener zest;

Seclusion oft the poison tongue attracts,

And scandal prospers on a dearth of facts.

'Twas said, the Sieur had more than once been spy'd

Alone at midnight by the river's side,

With aspect so uncouth, and gaze so strange,

That rustics cross'd themselves to see the change;

自光荣的往日留下骄傲的纪念；

但好奇的农夫们不断私下传闻

德布洛斯先生有别于其他的人。

此人又黑又瘦，有着光洁的头发，

并很少露出那一口闪亮的白牙，

他有尖锐的眼睛、暗中扫视的目光，

舌间温软甜美的法语快速奏响；

这位先生不被爱戴并少被目睹，

他总是难舍地待在自己的领土。

城堡的用人，稀少、谨慎又苍老，

本可以将许多诡秘的传说相告；

但年迈而驼背，他们很少走出大门

他们的父辈和祖先在此劳碌终身。

于是流言四起，而流言飞快传播，

当神秘导致了一种迫切的狂热；

离群索居常常将飞短流长引来，

而丑闻在真相不明时四处盛开。

据传，那位先生曾被数次看见

独自一人待在午夜时分的河畔，

露出粗野的外表，以及诡异的凝视，

乡民们为不再看到此景而画着十字；

Yet none, when press'd, could clearly say or know

Just what it was, or why they trembled so.

De Blois, as rumour whisper'd, fear'd to pray,

Nor us'd his chapel on the Sabbath day;

Howe'er this may have been, 'twas known at least

His household had no chaplain, monk, or priest.

But if the Master liv'd in dubious fame,

Twice fear'd and hated was his noble Dame;

As dark as he, in features wild and proud,

And with a weird supernal grace endow'd,

The haughty mistress scorn'd the rural train

Who sought to learn her source, but sought in vain.

Old women call'd her eyes too bright by half,

And nervous children shiver'd at her laugh;

Richard, the dwarf (whose word had little weight),

Vow'd she was like a serpent in her gait,

Whilst ancient Pierre (the aged often err)

Laid all her husband's mystery to her.

Still more absurd were those odd mutter'd things

That calumny to curious list'ners brings;

Those subtle slanders, told with downcast face,

但无人在催促下，能明确说出或知悉

那究竟是什么，他们又为何如此战栗。

德布洛斯，据流言所述，害怕祈祷，

也从不在安息日在他的教堂祷告；

不论这件事究竟如何，至少人所共知

他的住宅里没有教士、僧侣，或牧师。

而如果说这位大人有着可疑的声誉，

他高贵的女爵招致双倍的惧怕与恨意；

她也一样黝黑，有着野性傲慢的面目，

并且拥有某种怪异而又神圣的风度，

这位倨傲的女士对村民们报以轻慢

他们想了解她的出身，但却只是枉然。

年老的妇女说她有着太过明亮的眼睛，

而惶恐的孩子瑟瑟发抖于她的笑声。

矮人理查德（此人的话毫无分量），

发誓她的步态与一条蛇别无两样，

而年迈的皮埃尔（老得总是犯傻）

把她丈夫的一切谜团都归咎于她。

更荒唐的是那些反常的搬弄是非

在好奇的倾听者耳边散布诋毁；

那些狡猾的诽谤，被低垂的面庞讲述，

And muffled voice—those tales no man may trace;
Tales that the faith of old wives can command,
Tho' always heard at sixth or seventh hand.
Thus village legend darkly would imply
That Dame De Blois possess'd an evil eye;
Or going further, furtively suggest
A lurking spark of sorcery in her breast;
Old Mere Allard (herself half witch) once said
The lady's glance work'd strangely on the dead.
So liv'd the pair, like many another two
That shun the crowd, and shrink from public view.
They scorn'd the doubts by ev'ry peasant shewn,
And ask'd but one thing—to be let alone!

'Twas Candlemas [1], the dreariest time of year,
With fall long gone, and spring too far to cheer,
When little Jean, the bailiff's son and heir,
Fell sick and threw the doctors in despair.
A child so stout and strong that few would think
An hour might carry him to death's dark brink,
Yet pale he lay, tho' hidden was the cause,

---

1. Candlemas: 圣烛节，基督教节日，为纪念圣母玛利亚将耶
稣献给上帝而设，庆祝时间为每年的二月二日。

声音模糊不清——无人能将它们追溯；
这些传说令年迈的主妇们无比相信，
虽然经常在六七次转述后才被听闻。
于是村庄怪谈里含混地隐隐透漏
德布洛斯女爵有一只邪恶的眼球；
或者更进一步，藏头露尾地表明
有一片巫术火花潜伏在她的胸中；
阿拉德老嬷嬷（她算半个女巫）曾说
那位女士的视线对尸体有诡异的效果。
他们二人生活着，就像其他夫妻一样
他们躲开人群，并逃避着公众的目光。
他们蔑视每个农民显露出的猜疑，
只要求一件事情——能够不被干预！

在圣烛节，一年中最枯燥乏味之时，
秋天早已过去，远不是时候庆祝春日，
这时小吉恩，警官的儿子与继承者，
身染重病并使得医生们束手无策。
这孩子如此结实强壮所以人们不曾预见
他在转眼间就会陷入死亡阴暗的边缘，
他虚弱地躺着，但病因尚不清晰，

And Galens search'd in vain thro' Nature's laws.

But stricken sadness could not quite suppress

The roving thought, or wrinkled grandam's guess:

Tho' spoke by stealth, 'twas known to half a score

That Dame De Blois rode by the day before;

She had (they said) with glances weird and wild

Paus'd by the gate to view the prattling child,

Nor did they like the smile which seem'd to trace

New lines of evil on her proud, dark face.

These things they whisper'd, when the mother's cry

Told of the end—the gentle soul gone by;

In genuine grief the kindly watcher wept,

Whilst the lov'd babe with saints and angels slept.

The village priest his simple rites went thro',

And good Michel nail'd up the box of yew;

Around the corpse the holy candles burn'd,

The mourners sighed, the parents dumbly yearn'd.

Then one by one each sought his humble bed,

And left the lonely mother with her dead.

Late in the night it was, when o'er the vale

The storm-king swept with pandemoniac gale;

加伦斯徒劳地找寻着自然的规律。

但是苦闷的悲伤并不能够真正阻挡

流动的思绪，或是年迈老妪的猜想：

在低声密谈中，有十个人都知情

德布洛斯女爵曾在昨天骑马途经；

她（他们说）带着怪异又狂野的瞥视

停在了门前来看望胡言乱语的孩子，

那被众人所厌恶的微笑似乎正绘出

她傲慢黝黑的面庞上新的邪恶纹路。

当他们窃窃私语，母亲发出的哭泣

宣告了结束——柔弱的灵魂逝去；

慈祥的看护者带着真诚的忧伤流泪，

而被爱的孩子与圣徒和天使一同安睡。

村庄里的牧师举行了简单的仪式，

善人米歇尔将紫杉木的棺材钉死；

神圣的蜡烛围绕着尸体四周点燃，

吊唁者们叹息，而双亲默默地悼念。

随后人们一个个回到简陋的床铺，

留下孤单的母亲和亡子单独相处。

到了那一晚的深夜，在山谷上空

风暴之王扬起了喧嚣鼓噪的狂风；

Deep pil'd the cruel snow, yet strange to tell,
The lightning sputter'd while the white flakes fell;
A hideous presence seem'd abroad to steal,
And terror sounded in the thunder's peal.
Within the house of grief the tapers glow'd
Whilst the poor mother bow'd beneath her load;
Her salty eyes too tired now to weep,
Too pain'd to see, too sad to close in sleep.
The clock struck three. above the tempest heard
When something near the lifeless infant stirr'd.
Some slipp'ry thing, that flopp'd in awkward way,
And climb'd the table where the coffin lay;
With scaly convolutions strove to find
The cold, still clay that death had left behind.
The nodding mother hears—starts broad awake—
Empower'd to reason, yet too stunn'd to shake;
The pois'nous thing she sees, and nimbly foils
The ghoulish purpose of the quiv'ring coils:
With ready axe the serpent's head she cleaves,
And thrills with savage triumph whilst she grieves.
The injur'd reptile hissing glides from sight,

严酷的积雪厚厚堆起，说来奇特，

白色的雪花落下时伴着闪电大作；

一种丑恶的存在似乎在室外潜伏，

而在雷霆的轰鸣之中传来了恐怖。

在那间烛火闪耀的忧伤房屋之内

可怜的母亲在重负之下弯起后背；

她苦涩的眼睛已经疲倦得无法哭泣，

痛苦得盲目，又悲伤得无法睡去。

时钟敲击三下，回响在暴风雨中

死去的孩子身旁有东西蠢蠢欲动。

那光滑的东西，以笨拙的移动方式，

爬上了那张放置着棺木的桌子；

带着盘卷的鳞片奋力地找寻

死亡所留下的冰冷平静的尸身。

打盹的母亲听见——很快睡意全消——

恢复了理智，但震惊得忘了颤抖；

她看到那个毒物，并且机敏地阻拦

那抖动的盘蛇怀有的阴险的打算：

她用准备的斧子劈向了毒蛇的头，

在悲伤之余因野蛮的胜利而颤抖。

受伤的爬虫嘶嘶地滑出了视野，

And hides its cloven carcass in the night.

The weeks slipp'd by, and gossip's tongue began
To call the Sieur De Blois an alter'd man;
With curious mien he oft would pace along
The village street, and eye the gaping throng.
Yet whilst he shew'd himself as ne'er before,
His wild-eyed lady was observ'd no more.
In course of time, 'twas scarce thought odd or ill
That he his ears with village lore should fill;
Nor was the town with special rumour rife
When he sought out the bailiff and his wife:
Their tale of sorrow, with its ghastly end,
Was told, indeed, by ev'ry wond'ring friend.
The Sieur heard all, and low'ring rode away,
Nor was he seen again for many a day.

When vernal sunshine shed its cheering glow,
And genial zephyrs blew away the snow,
To frighten'd swains a horror was reveal'd
In the damp herbage of a melting field.

并把自己裂开的尸体藏匿于黑夜。

一周周过去，流言蜚语中声称
德布洛斯先生已经有所不同；
他常常带着探寻的神态独自行进
在村里的街道，扫视惊讶的人群。
而当他像这样前所未有地抛头露面，
他双眼圆睁的夫人再也没有被看见。
久而久之，不再有怪异病态的猜测
传入他充斥着乡间传闻的耳朵；
村庄里也没有再盛行新的谣诼
当他最后将警官夫妇二人查到：
他们悲惨的故事，与可怕的结局，
着实被每个诧异的朋友不断提起。
先生听闻这一切，阴沉地骑马上路，
自此很多天再也没有被人们目睹。

当春季的阳光将欢快的光芒照映，
而温煦的和风将积雪席卷一空，
惊恐的农夫们面前有着恐怖展现
于融雪的田野上潮湿的牧草里面。

There (half preserv'd by winter's frigid bed)
Lay the dark Dame De Blois, untimely dead;
By some assassin's stroke most foully slain,
Her shapely brow and temples cleft in twain.
Reluctant hands the dismal burden bore
To the stone arches of the husband's door,
Where silent serfs the ghastly thing receiv'd,
Trembling with fright, but less amaz'd than griev'd;
The Sieur his dame beheld with blazing eyes
And shook with anger, more than with surprise.
(At least 'tis thus the stupid peasants told
Their wide-mouth'd wives when they the tale unroll'd.)
The village wonder'd why De Blois had kept
His spouse's loss unmention'd and unwept,
Nor were there lacking sland'rous tongues to claim
That the dark master was himself to blame.
But village talk could scarcely hope to solve
A crime so deep, and thus the months revolve:
The rural train repeat the gruesome tale,
And gape and marvel more than they bewail.

那里（被冬日寒冷的卧床所保留）

躺着黝黑的德布洛斯女爵，不知死了多久；

被某个刺客的一击无比卑劣地杀害，

她匀称的额头与太阳穴向两侧裂开。

无奈的手掌承担着这阴沉的负重

运送至她丈夫门前的石质门拱，

那里沉默的奴隶接过可怕的东西，

因恐惧而颤抖，但忧伤多于诧异；

先生用炽热的双眼将他的女爵观察

因愤怒而颤抖，而并非只是惊讶。

（至少愚笨的农夫们是这样告知

他们长舌的妻子，当谈起这个故事。）

整个村子好奇德布洛斯为何掩藏

从不提起或悼念他配偶的死亡，

并非没有恶意中伤的谣言宣说

那位暗黑的领主该为事情负责。

但是乡间的传言根本不可能解决

至深的罪恶，于是过去了数月：

村里的人们将这可怕的故事复述，

相比于哀悼他们总是张口瞪目。

Swift flew the sun, and winter once again
With icy talons gripp'd the frigid plain.
December brought its store of Christmas cheer,
And grateful peasants hail'd the op'ning year;
But by the hearth as Candlemas drew nigh,
The whisp'ring ancients spoke of things gone by.
Few had forgot the dark demoniac lore
Of things that came the Candlemas before,
And many a crone intently eyed the house
Where dwelt the sadden'd bailiff and his spouse.
At last the day arriv'd, the sky o'erspread
With dark'ning messengers and clouds of lead;
Each neighb'ring grove Aeolian warnings sigh'd,
And thick'ning terrors broadcast seem'd to bide.
The good folk, tho' they knew not why, would run
Swift past the bailiff's door, the scene to shun;
Within the house the grieving couple wept,
And mourn'd the child who now forever slept.
On rush'd the dusk in doubly hideous form,
Borne on the pinions of the gath'ring storm;
Unusual murmurs fill'd the rainless wind,

日影快速滑过，又是一个冬天
冰冷的利爪握紧了严寒的平原。
十二月带来了丰裕的圣诞欢乐，
感恩的农民们为新的一年庆贺；
但炉火旁边随着圣烛节的临近，
低语的老人将过去的事情议论。
没有人忘记昏暗的魔鬼般的传说中
在上一个圣烛节发生的那些事情，
而许多老妪专注地看着那间房屋
悲伤的警官夫妻仍在那里居住。
最后当那天到来，天空中覆盖
阴沉的预兆和铅一样的云彩；
附近每片树丛呼啸着风中的警告，
浓厚的恐惧似乎等待着得到播报。
好人们，虽然不知何故，会奔跑着
快速经过警官的门口，避开这个场所；
悲痛的夫妇正在房屋里面流泪，
哀悼着他们的孩子永远陷入沉睡。
在黄昏时涌现了更加丑恶的影迹，
被承载于凝聚的风暴的羽翼；
无雨的风被异常的呢喃充斥，

And hast'ning trav'llers fear'd to glance behind.
Mad o'er the hills the daemon tempest tore;
The rising river lash'd the troubled shore;
Black thro' the night the awful storm-god prowl'd,
And froze the list'ners' life-blood as he howl'd;
Gigantic trees like supple rushes sway'd,
Whilst for his home the trembling cotter pray'd.
Now falls a sudden lull amidst the gale;
With less'ning force the circling currents wail;
Far down the stream that laves the neighb'ring mead
Burst a new ululation, wildly key'd;
The peasant train a frantic mien assume,
And huddle closer in the spectral gloom:
To each strain'd ear the truth too well is known,
For that dread sound can come from wolves alone!
The rustics close attend, when ere they think,
A lupine army swarms the river's brink;
From out the waters leap a howling train
That rend the air, and scatter o'er the plain:
With flaming orbs the frothing creatures fly,
And chant with hellish voice their hungry cry.

匆匆的行人不敢向身后窥视。

恶魔般的暴雨疯狂地高踞群山；

暴涨的河流拍击着忧郁的海岸；

可怕的风暴之神阴沉地徘徊于黑夜，

用他的怒吼冻结了聆听者的心血；

高大的树木如柔韧的灯芯草般飘摇，

而颤抖的佃农为他的房屋所祈祷。

此刻在风中突然降临了一丝平和；

回旋的气流的哭泣也变得微弱；

在那流经附近草地的小溪远处

爆发出一阵音调狂野的高呼；

农夫的队伍将慌乱的表情显现，

并在幽灵般的黑暗中挤成一团：

每一个紧张的耳朵都深深明白真相，

这可怕的声音只能够来自恶狼！

村民们上前查看，不等他们思考，

一支狼群大军就从河岸周围包抄；

这支呼啸的队列在水边奔跳而来

撕裂了空气，并在平原之上散开：

双眼血红、口吐白沫的生物飞速前行，

并用可憎的声音反复发出饥渴的长鸣。

First of the pack a mighty monster leaps

With fearless tread, and martial order keeps;

Th' attendant wolves his yelping tones obey

And form in columns for the coming fray:

No frighten'd swain they harm, but silent bound

With a fix'd purpose o'er the frozen ground.

Straight course the monsters thro' the village street,

Unholy vigour in their flying feet;

Thro' half-shut blinds the shelter'd peasants peer,

And wax in wonder as they lose in fear.

Th' excited pack at last their goal perceive,

And the vex'd air with deaf'ning clamour cleave;

The churls, astonish'd, watch th' unnatural herd

Flock round a cottage at the leader's word:

Quick spreads the fearsome fact, by rumour blown,

That the doom'd cottage is the bailiff's own!

Round and around the howling daemons glide,

Whilst the fierce leader scales the vine-clad side;

The frantic wind its horrid wail renews,

And mutters madly thro' the lifeless yews.

In the frail house the bailiff calmly waits

兽群中领头的强大怪物一跃而起

有着无畏的步伐，与军人般的纪律；

随从的群狼将他尖叫的声音谨守

并分成小队，以备即将到来的恶斗：

它们未伤害恐惧的村民，沉默地跳跃

在这冰冻的地表之上目标明确。

这群怪物直奔村里的街道而去，

飞奔的步伐中带有不洁的活力；

躲藏的农夫透过半掩的窗帘窥看，

在逐渐好奇的同时于恐惧中深陷。

最后振奋的兽群发现了它们的目标，

在烦恼的空气中传来喧哗的吵闹；

震惊的村夫们看到这怪异的团队

遵首领命令将一幢小屋团团包围：

可怕的真相很快流传，按流言所说，

这座万劫不复的小屋正是警官那座！

这群嗥叫的恶魔飞掠着绕个不停，

凶悍的首领沿青藤覆盖的墙面攀登；

狂躁的风重新开始了骇人的哭喊，

疯狂地低语着穿过枯死的紫杉。

在脆弱的房屋中警官平静地等待

The rav'ning horde, and trusts th' impartial Fates,
But the wan wife revives with curious mien
Another monster and an older scene;
Amidst th' increasing wind that rocks the walls,
The dame to him the serpent's deed recalls:
Then as a nameless thought fills both their minds,
The bare-fang'd leader crashes thro' the blinds.
Across the room, with murd'rous fury rife,
Leaps the mad wolf, and seizes on the wife;
With strange intent he drags his shrieking prey
Close to the spot where once the coffin lay.
Wilder and wilder roars the mounting gale
That sweeps the hills and hurtles thro' the vale;
The ill-made cottage shakes, the pack without
Dance with new fury in demoniac rout.
Quick as his thought, the valiant bailiff stands
Above the wolf, a weapon in his hands;
The ready axe that serv'd a year before,
Now serves as well to slay one monster more.
The creature drops inert, with shatter'd head,
Full on the floor, and silent as the dead;

凶猛的敌群，并相信命运的仲裁，
但苍白的妻子神情怪异地追溯
另一只怪物与曾经发生的一幕；
在摇撼着墙壁的愈加强烈的风里，
女爵蛇一样的行为唤起他的回忆：
当莫名的思绪充斥着他们的脑海，
露出利齿的头狼从窗帘冲了进来。
穿过了房间，满怀着凶残的狂怒，
疯狂的狼飞跃过来将妻子抓住；
他居心叵测地将尖叫的猎物拉扯
直至曾经放置着棺材的那个场所。
激增的狂风愈加狂野地怒吼
飞驰在山谷并且横扫过山丘；
凶险的小屋摇晃着，门外的兽群
带着狂怒舞动并着魔一般飞奔。
转念之间，英勇的警官站立于
头狼上方，手里拿着一把武器；
那把在一年前大显神威的利斧，
现在同样要发威杀死另一只怪物。
那生物无力地倒下，脑袋被击破，
填满了地面，像死去一样沉默；

The rescu'd wife recalls the dire alarms,

And faints from terror in her husband's arms.

But as he holds her, all the cottage quakes,

And with full force the titan tempest breaks:

Down crash the walls, and o'er their shrinking forms

Burst the mad revels of the storm of storms.

Th' encircling wolves advance with ghastly pace,

Hunger and murder in each gleaming face,

But as they close, from out the hideous night

Flashes a bolt of unexpected light:

The vivid scene to ev'ry eye appears,

And peasants shiver with returning fears.

Above the wreck the scatheless chimney stays,

Its outline glimm'ring in the fitful rays,

Whilst o'er the hearth still hangs the household shrine,

The Saviour's image and the Cross divine!

Round the blest spot a lambent radiance glows,

And shields the cotters from their stealthy foes:

Each monstrous creature marks the wondrous glare,

Drops, fades, and vanishes in empty air!

The village train with startled eyes adore,

获救的妻子取消了危险的警报，

并出于恐惧晕倒在她丈夫的怀抱。

但当他拥紧她，整座小屋都在战栗，

巨型的暴风雨终于竭尽全力来袭：

墙壁在坍塌，落向他们畏缩的面颊

风暴之风将那疯狂的庆典爆发。

那环绕的狼群以可怖的速度前进，

每张闪烁的脸上带着饥渴与祸心，

但当它们接近，从那丑恶的夜幕

射下了一道猝不及防的闪电光束：

清晰的景象显现在每个人眼前，

农民们因再度降临的恐惧发颤。

仅有完好的烟囱矗立在废墟之上，

它的轮廓被断断续续的光芒照亮，

家里的神龛仍然在壁炉之上悬挂，

有着救主的画像和神圣的十字架！

在这降福的地点旁有一束光线摇曳，

将村中众人与他们隐匿的敌人隔绝：

每只凶残的生物看到这奇异的光线，

都倒地，褪色，在空气中消失不见！

村里的众人用吃惊的目光表示诚服，

And count their beads in rev'rence o'er and o'er.
Now fades the light, and dies the raging blast,
The hour of dread and reign of horror past.
Pallid and bruis'd, from out his toppled walls
The panting bailiff with his good wife crawls:
Kind hands attend them, whilst o'er all the town
A strange sweet peace of spirit settles down.
Wonder and fear are still'd in soothing sleep,
As thro' the breaking clouds the moon rays peep.

Here paus'd the prattling grandam in her speech,
Confus'd with age, the tale half out of reach;
The list'ning guest, impatient for a clue,
Fears 'tis not one tale, but a blend of two;
He fain would know how far'd the widow'd lord
Whose eerie ways th' initial theme afford,
And marvels that the crone so quick should slight
His fate, to babble of the wolf-wrack'd night.
The old wife, press'd, for greater clearness strives,
Nods wisely, and her scatter'd wits revives;
Yet strangely lingers on her latter tale

他们满怀着崇敬一遍又一遍祷祝。
此刻光芒熄灭，狂暴的轰鸣平息，
惊骇的时刻与恐怖的统治都已过去。
苍白而负伤，从那堆倾覆的墙壁下
气喘吁吁的警官与爱妻向外攀爬：
友善的手掌迎接他们，而整座村庄
都迎来了奇异甜美的心灵的安详。
疑惑与恐惧在安宁的睡眠中缓和，
明月的光辉透过散开的云层照射。

唠唠叨叨的老妇将故事在此打住，
高龄而昏聩，另一半变得遥不可触；
聆听的客人，热切地期待着线索，
担心这并非一个传说，而是两者混合；
他想要知道丧妻的领主后来的进展
他怪异的行事被最初的主题表现，
并奇怪于为何老妇会轻易地忽略
他的命运，去讲述恶狼成灾的黑夜。
老妇人受到催促，力求讲得更清楚，
智慧地点头，而她零散的心智复苏；
于是她剩余的故事得以奇妙地延续

Of wolf and bailiff, miracle and gale.

When (quoth the crone) the dawn's bright radiance bath'd

Th' eventful scene, so late in terror swath'd,

The chatt'ring churls that sought the ruin'd cot

Found a new marvel in the gruesome spot.

From fallen walls a trail of gory red,

As of the stricken wolf, erratic led;

O'er road and mead the new-dript crimson wound,

Till lost amidst the neighb'ring swampy ground:

With wonder unappeas'd the peasants burn'd,

For what the quicksand takes is ne'er return'd.

Once more the grandam, with a knowing eye,

Stops in her tale, to watch a hawk soar by;

The weary list'ner, baffled, seeks anew

For some plain statement, or enlight'ning clue.

Th' indulgent crone attends the puzzled plea,

Yet strangely mutters o'er the mystery.

The Sieur? Ah, yes—that morning all in vain

His shaking servants scour'd the frozen plain;

No man had seen him since he rode away

关于恶狼与警官，狂风与奇迹。
当（按老妇所说）黎明的光辉照耀
那多事之地，不久前被恐惧笼罩，
交头接耳的村民将小屋的废墟巡视
并在那可怕的地方发现了新的怪事。
在颓圮的墙下一条血淋淋的印痕，
似来自受伤的狼，不规则地延伸；
这条崭新的赤色血迹穿过道路与草坪，
直到消失在附近沼泽的地面当中：
无法满足的好奇在农夫们心中点燃，
因为被泥潭吞噬之物再也不会重现。

再一次那位老妇，闪着知情的眼睛，
停下了她的故事，仰望翱翔的雄鹰；
疲惫的倾听者，疑惑地，重新呼吁
一些直白的说明，或线索的启迪。
宽容的老妇倾听了迷茫的请愿，
用诡秘的喃喃低语谈论起疑团。
那位先生？啊，是的——那个徒劳的早晨
他颤抖的仆人们将冰冷的原野搜寻；
没有人看到他自从他骑马离去

In silence on the dark preceding day,
His horse, wild-eyed with some unusual fright,
Came wand'ring from the river-bank that night.
His hunting-hound, that mourn'd with piteous woe,
Howl'd by the quicksand swamp, his grief to shew.
The village folk thought much, but utter'd less;
The servants search wore out in emptiness:
For Sieur De Blois (the old wife's tale is o'er)
Was lost to mortal sight for evermore.

在那个黑暗的前夕不发一语。

他的马，因异常的恐惧双眼大开，

在那个夜晚从河岸旁游荡而来。

他的猎犬，带着痛惜的悲伤悼念，

在泥潭沼泽旁吠叫，显示出他的哀怨。

村民们想了很多，却议论甚少；

仆人们竭力的搜寻最终只是徒劳：

因为德布洛斯先生（老妇的传说完结）

从此再也没有出现在人们的视野。

幻灵
The Eidolon

发表于《试验》1918 年十月刊。

'Twas at a nameless hour of night
When fancies in delirious flight
About the silent sleeper reel
And thro' his mindless visions steal;
When flesh upon its earthly bed
Sprawls corpse-like and untenanted—
Vacant of soul, which freely flies
Thro' worlds unknown to waking eyes.
The horned moon above the spire
With ghastly grace was crawling high'r,
And in the pallid struggling beams
Grinn'd memories of ancient dreams.
Aloft in heav'n each starry sign
Flicker'd fantastic and malign,
Whilst voices from the gaping deep
Bade me assuage my woes in sleep.
This scene, one night in chill November,
I shall thro' many a year remember.
Beneath another moon I espy'd

那是夜里的一个无名时刻

当幻影在极度兴奋中飞过

在沉默的睡眠者身边环绕

并潜入他失去意识的视角；

当肉体在它世俗的卧床上

尸体一样无人问津地伸张——

空闲的灵魂，自由地飞行

穿越清醒之眼未知的时空。

尖塔之上号角一般的弯月

带着可怖的优雅向上攀越，

而在苍白又扭曲的光束里

冷笑着远古的梦境的回忆。

高踞于上苍的每一个星座

在不可思议地恶毒地闪烁，

而裂开的深渊中传出音声

吩咐我将梦中的悲伤抚平。

此景，十一月寒冷的一晚，

我将在很多年后将它纪念。

在另一轮月下我远远望及

A bleak and barren countryside,

Where spectral shadows darkly crept

O'er moorland mounds where dead things slept.

The beck'ning moonlight wanly play'd

On forms unusual and ill-made,

Aerial forms from strange dominions,

Hither and thither borne on pinions

That flutter'd as in fev'rish quest

Of some far land of light and rest.

In this dark throng my sight could trace

Beings from all ethereal space;

A sentient chaos gather'd here

From ev'ry immemorial sphere,

Yet of one mind, with ardour rife

To find the Eidolon call'd **Life** [1].

The murky moon, a daemon eye

Drunkenly winking in the sky,

Flew on and on above the plain

And drew my spirit in its train.

I saw a mountain, coronate

With cities populous and great,

---

1. The Eidolon call'd Life: 化用自爱伦·坡《梦境》中的诗句 "an Eidolon, named Night"。

一片萧瑟荒凉的乡村地区，
那里幢幢的鬼影暗中游走
越过死物沉睡的沼地山丘。
诱惑的月光正惨白地照映
不同寻常而又病态的身影，
从异界涌出的飘飞的影迹，
被羽翼所承载着忽来忽去
飞舞时如同在狂热地追逐
某处光明平静的遥远沃土。
我眼中发现这黑暗的集团
当中的生物来自异星空间；
聚集于此的有知觉的混沌
从每个上古的星球上降临，
却目标一致，满带着激情
搜寻着被称作**人生**的幻灵。
朦胧的月亮，如恶魔之眼
醉醺醺地眨动在夜空上面，
高飞在平原之上连绵不绝
将我的灵魂卷入它的行列。
我看到一座山岳，在顶峰
有宏伟而人口众多的高城，

Whose habitants, a mighty number,
Lay hid in deep nocturnal slumber,
So that the moon for long dim hours
Leer'd on lone streets and silent tow'rs.
Fair beyond words the mountain stood,
Its base encircled by a wood;
Adown its side a brooklet bright
Ran dancing in the spectral light.
Each city that adorn'd its crest
Seem'd anxious to outvie the rest,
For carven columns, domes, and fanes
Gleam'd rich and lovely o'er the plains.
And now the moon in heav'n stood still
As if no more foreboding ill,
Whereat the throngs aërial knew
That **Life** at last was in their view;
That the fair mount each gaz'd upon
Was **Life**, the long-sought Eidolon!
But lo! what rays the scene illume
As dawn intrudes upon the gloom?
The East is hideous with the flare

它的居民，数量极为庞大，

藏入夜间深邃的沉睡之下，

而月光在昏暗的时刻久久

睨视着孤街和沉寂的塔楼。

这耸立之山美得不可言喻，

它的山脚被一片树林围起；

一条澄澈小溪沿山腰流淌

跃动时有着幽灵般的光芒。

点缀着山顶的每一座城市

似乎都在渴望着超越彼此，

雕花的圆柱、穹顶，与寺院

可爱又众多地显现于地面。

此刻高空的明月静静停顿

似乎不会再有不祥的厄运，

而那些纷飞的群体们知晓

人生最后终于被它们看到；

各自眼中那座美丽的山峰

是**人生**，寻找已久的幻灵！

看！何等的光辉照亮此地

当黎明从上方闯入了阴郁？

在东方触目惊心地闪烁着

Of blood-hued light—a garish glare—
While ghastly grey the mountain stands,
The terror of the neighb'ring lands.
The cursed wood of twisted trees
Waves awful talons in the breeze,
And down the slope the oozing stream
Reflects the day with shocking gleam.
Aloft the light of knowledge crawls,
Staining the crumbling city walls
Thro' hich in troops ungainly squirm
The foetid lizard and the worm.
White leprous marble in the light
Shews sculptures that repel and fright,
And many a temple hints the sin
And blasphemy that reign within.
"O Pow'rs of Light and Space and Aidenn [1] ,
Is **Life** with such foul horrors laden?
Pray hide no more the wondrous plan,
But shew the living glory—Man!"
Now on the streets the houses spew
A loathsome pestilence, a crew

---

1. Aidenn: 伊甸的另一种拼写方式。本词在爱伦·坡的诗歌中频频出现。

血色的光芒——耀眼的怒火——

而山峰灰暗又可怖地高耸，

为四周的土地带去了惊恐。

诅咒森林之中扭曲的树木

如可怖的利爪般随风挥舞，

而顺坡流淌的浑浊的溪流

倒映出惊颤地闪烁的白昼。

知识之光爬过更高的地方，

玷污了城市中颓圮的高墙

在它里面丑恶地成群蠕动

是散发着恶臭的蜥蜴蛆虫。

光芒下不洁的白色大理石

将可憎又骇人的雕塑展示，

而众多的寺院暗示着惩罪

它们的内部被亵渎所支配。

"哦，光明宇宙以及天国之力，

难道**人生**充满污秽的恐惧？

请不要再掩藏奇妙的剧本，

展现出活生生的荣耀——人！"

此刻街道上的房屋里吐出

令人作呕的毒物，是一组

Of things I cannot, dare not name,

So vile their form, so black their shame.

And in the sky the leering sun

Laughs at the havock he hath done,

Nor pities the vague forms that flee

Back to the Night eternally.

*"O Moonlit, Mound-mark'd Moor of **Death**,*

Renew thy reign! Thy lethal breath

Is balm elysian to the soul

That sees the light and knows the whole."

I sought to join the winged train

That plung'd into the dusk again,

But Horror, eating at my mind,

Held my poor falt'ring steps behind.

In dreams I fain would flee the day—

Too late, for I have lost the way!

我无法又不敢命名的东西，

乃丑陋之至，又可耻之极。

而天空之中睨视着的太阳

取乐于被他所降下的灾殃，

毫不怜悯逃走的模糊身影

撤回到那永恒的黑夜之中。

"哦，月下与山边的**死亡**荒地，

再度统治吧！你致命的吹息

对灵魂来说是极乐的安抚

它们看到光明并知道全部。"

我想要加入那有翼的族群

随它们再一次投身于黄昏，

但恐惧，蚕食着我的心智，

将我可悲迟疑的脚步阻止。

梦中我多想从这一天逃亡——

太迟了，我已迷失了方向！

A Cycle of Verse

组诗

《海洋之神》与《云朵》发表于 1919 年 3 月 20
日的《国家询问报》，《大地母亲》发表于 1919 年 3
月 27 日的《国家询问报》。

海洋之神
Oceanus

海洋之神，音译为俄亥阿诺斯或欧申纳斯，希腊神话中所有海神与河神的始祖。

Sometimes I stand upon the shore
Where ocean vaults their effluence pour,
And troubled waters sigh and shriek
Of secrets that they dare not speak.
From nameless valleys far below,
And hills and plains no man may know,
The mystic swells and sullen surges
Hint like accursed thaumaturges
A thousand horrors, big with awe,
That long-forgotten ages saw.
O salt, salt winds, that bleakly sweep
Across the barren heaving deep:
O wild, wan waves, that call to mind
The chaos Earth hath left behind:
Of you I ask one thing alone—
Leave, leave your ancient lore unknown!

有时候我独自站在海岸之旁
海洋的穹顶在此将激流簸扬，
忧郁的苦水哀鸣中带有叹息
只因它们不敢提起那些秘密。
从那片远在下方的无名谷口，
直到不为人知的平原与山丘，
那神秘的溢流与阴沉的波涛
如同受诅的魔法师降下预兆
千般的恐怖，被畏惧所充满，
曾被目睹于久已遗忘的纪元。
哦，咸涩的海风阴冷地吹拂
穿过向下延伸至深处的荒芜：
哦，汹涌的雪浪呼唤着内心
被大地所遗留下的一片混沌：
对于你我只愿祈求一件事情——
将你那古老的知识守口如瓶！

云朵
Clouds

Of late I climb'd a lonely height
And watch'd the moon-streak'd clouds in flight,
Whose forms fantastic reel'd and whirl'd
Like genii of a spectral world.
Thin cirri veil'd the silv'ry dome
And waver'd like the ocean foam,
While shapes of darker, heavier kind
Scudded before a daemon wind.
Methought the churning vapours took
Now and anon a fearsome look,
As if amidst the fog and blur
March'd figures known and sinister.
From west to east the things advanc'd—
A mocking train that leap'd and danc'd
Like Bacchanals with joined hands
In endless file thro' airy lands.
Aerial mutt'rings, dimly heard,
The comfort of my spirit stirr'd
With hideous thoughts, that bade me screen
My sight from the portentous scene.
"Yon fleeting mists," the murmurs said,
"Are ghosts of hopes, deny'd and dead."

云朵

不久前我独自向着高处攀登

仰望月光下的云朵高高飞腾，

它们奇妙的形体盘绕并旋转

如同虚幻世界中的灯神一般。

稀疏的卷云将银色天穹遮罩

并像海洋中的泡沫一样飘摇，

而另一些昏暗、浓密的影迹

随着恶魔之风一同飞掠而去。

我眼中那些翻腾不息的云雾

不时将一张可怕的面容展露，

似乎就在朦胧与雾气的中央

成排行进着熟悉的不祥影像。

那些存在自西向东逐渐迈进——

一支跳跃并起舞的讥诮大军

如狂欢作乐者一般双手联合

以无尽的队列穿过空气之国。

空中的低语声，隐约间传来，

我灵魂之中的慰藉开始澎湃

那些恶毒的思绪，吩咐我隔绝

虚有其表的景象前这片视野。

"那些过眼烟云，"低语声告知，

"是希望之灵，挫败并已消逝。"

大地母亲
Mother Earth

One night I wander'd down the bank
Of a deep valley, hush'd and dank,
Whose stagnant air possess'd a taint
And chill that made me sick and faint.
The frequent trees on ev'ry hand
Loom'd like a ghastly goblin[1] band,
And branches'gainst the narrowing sky
Took shapes I fear'd—I knew not why.
Deeper I plung'd, and seem'd to grope
For some lost thing as joy or hope,
Yet found, for all my searchings there,
Naught save the phantoms of despair.
The walls contracted as I went
Still farther in my mad descent,
Till soon, of moon and stars bereft,
I crouch'd within a rocky cleft
So deep and ancient that the stone
Breath'd things primordial and unknown.
My hands, exploring, strove to trace

---

1. goblin: 地精，又译哥布林，西方奇幻传说中身材矮小的绿
皮亚人生物，生性狡猾邪恶。

一天夜里我从岸边漫步穿行
幽深的山谷，寂静而又阴冷，
它沉滞的空气中充满了腐臭
与寒意，使得我晕眩而作呕。
每一个方向上密布着的树林
显现得如同可憎的地精族群，
而枝条向着狭窄的天空伸出
形状令我害怕——我不知何故。
我逐渐深入，似乎想要探索
某些久已失落的希望与欢乐，
却察觉，在此我所有的发现
只有毫无价值的绝望的虚幻。
崖壁随着我的前行逐渐收紧
当我在疯狂下行中愈陷愈深，
很快，月亮与群星消隐无形，
我俯身踏入了一条岩间裂缝
如此幽深古老以至那些顽石
吐露着悠久而又未知的往事。
我的双手，摸索着努力寻找

The features of the valley's face,
When midst the gloom they seem'd to find
An outline frightful to my mind.
Not any shape my straining eyes,
Could they have seen, might recognise;
For what I touch'd bespoke a day
Too old for man's fugacious sway.
The clinging lichens moist and hoary
Forbade me read the antique story;
But hidden water, trickling low,
Whisper'd the tales I should not know.
"Mortal, ephemeral and bold,
In mercy keep what I have told,
Yet think sometimes of what hath been,
And sights these crumbling rocks have seen;
Of sentience old ere thy weak brood
Appear'd in lesser magnitude,
And living things that yet survive,
Tho' not to human ken alive.
I AM THE VOICE OF MOTHER EARTH,
FROM WHENCE ALL HORRORS HAVE THEIR BIRTH."

山谷的面庞具有的那些形貌，

而阴暗笼罩下它们似乎寻获

一条使得我心惊胆战的轮廓。

那些形状对于我受限的视界，

哪怕还能目睹，也不能辨别；

因为我触及之物成形的时间

相比人的短暂统治太过久远。

上面依附的青苔湿润又陈腐

使我无法将远古的故事阅读；

但隐秘的流水，在下方淅沥，

将我本不该知道的传说低语。

"凡人，稍纵即逝却如此胆大，

将我满怀着仁慈的话语记下，

时常想一想曾经发生的过往，

与坍塌的岩石曾看到的景象；

那感觉先于你们弱小的种族

在微不足道之中突然间冒出，

而那些生灵在此刻仍然存在，

却处于人类有生的视线之外。

正在对你发声者是大地母亲，

所有的恐怖全部因我而降临。"

绝望
Despair

发表于《松果》1919 年六月刊。本诗是洛夫克拉夫特在母亲身患恶疾之时所作。

O'er the midnight moorlands crying,
Thro' the cypress forests sighing,
In the night-wind madly flying,
    Hellish forms with streaming hair;
In the barren branches creaking,
By the stagnant swamp-pools speaking,
Past the shore-cliffs ever shrieking;
    Damn'd daemons of despair.

Once, I think I half remember,
Ere the grey skies of November
Quench'd my youth's aspiring ember,
    Liv'd there such a thing as bliss;
Skies that now are dark were beaming,
Gold and azure, splendid seeming
Till I learn'd it all was dreaming—
    Deadly drowsiness of Dis[1].

---

1. Dis: 狄斯，罗马神话中的冥王。

在午夜中哭泣的沼地上面，

穿越柏树森林发出的悲叹，

于疯狂飞翔着的夜风之间，

　　有群毛发飘扬的可憎形象；

嘎吱作响的枯瘦枝条之内，

发出低语的污秽沼泽周围，

尖叫不止的海岸悬崖山背；

　　那些受诅的恶魔象征绝望。

曾经，我自以为模糊地记起，

当十一月的灰暗天空未及

将我青春激情的余烬吹熄，

　　至福仍存在于那段时间；

如今昏黑的天空曾放出光芒，

金黄又蔚蓝，看起来灿烂辉煌

直到我发觉这一切只是空想——

　　是来自冥王的致命沉眠。

But the stream of Time, swift flowing,
Brings the torment of half-knowing—
Dimly rushing, blindly going
    Past the never-trodden lea;
And the voyager, repining,
Sees the wicked death-fires shining,
Hears the wicked petrel's whining
    As he helpless drifts to sea.

Evil wings in ether beating;
Vultures at the spirit eating;
Things unseen forever fleeting
    Black against the leering sky.
Ghastly shades of bygone gladness,
Clawing fiends of future sadness,
Mingle in a cloud of madness
    Ever on the soul to lie.

Thus the living, lone and sobbing,
In the throes of anguish throbbing,
With the loathsome Furies [1] *robbing*

---

1. Furies: 弗里斯，希腊神话中提西福涅、阿勒克托、墨盖拉三位复仇女神的总称。

但是时间之河飞速地流动，

带来令人难以尽知的苦痛——

昏暗地奔腾，盲目地前行

　　穿过了无人涉足的草地；

而那位航行者满腹牢骚，

眼前邪恶的死火正在闪耀，

耳边响起海燕邪恶的哭嚎

　　当他无助地向大海漂去。

邪恶的羽翼在以太中振翅；

秃鹰们在灵魂的上方暴食；

永不可见的事物转瞬即逝

　　在睨视的天空留下黑影。

旧日欢乐留下可怖的阴霾，

未来之悲化作利爪的鬼怪，

在疯狂的云雾中混杂开来

　　压迫在心灵上从始至终。

于是孤单而充满泪水的生活，

随着苦楚的剧痛的阵阵发作，

被令人厌恶的弗里斯夺走了

Night and noon of peace and rest.
But beyond the groans and grating
Of abhorrent Life, is waiting
Sweet Oblivion, culminating
All the years of fruitless quest.

宁静安详的正午和黑夜。

但越过了呻吟和噪声之后

可憎的生命，那里等候有

甜美的湮灭，它将会停休

无功追寻中的漫长岁月。

揭示
Revelation

发表于《试验》1919 年三月刊。

In a vale of light and laughter,
Smiling 'neath the friendly sun,
Where fulfilment follow'd after
Ev'ry hope or dream begun;
Where an Aidenn gay and glorious,
Beckon'd down the winsome way;
There my soul, o'er pain victorious,
Laugh'd and lingered—yesterday.

Green and narrow was my valley,
Temper'd with a verdant shade;
Sun deck'd brooklets musically
Sparkled thro' each glorious glade;
And at night the stars serenely
Glow'd betwixt the boughs o'erhead,
While Astarte [1], calm and queenly,
Floods of fairy radiance shed.

---

1. Astarte: 阿施塔特，迦南人和腓尼基人信奉的女神，掌管丰收、生育、战争。

有座山谷充满欢笑与光辉，

在和暖的阳光下露出笑容，

那里如愿以偿会紧紧跟随

每一个希望和梦想的诞生；

那里有着欢愉壮丽的天国，

被召唤着穿过迷人的路线；

我的灵魂成功将苦痛超脱，

欢笑并流连着——皆在昨天。

我那座山谷狭小而又葱郁；

在青翠的色调中无比安详；

阳光点缀的河水奏起旋律

闪烁着穿越每处林间空旷；

夜晚之中那些宁静的星斗

在头顶上方的枝叶间闪耀，

而阿施塔特，平静如皇后

将潮水般美丽的光芒映照。

There amid the tinted bowers,
Raptur'd with the opiate spell
Of the grasses, ferns and flowers,
Poppy, Phlox and Pimpernel,
Long I lay, entranc'd and dreaming,
Pleas'd with Nature's bounteous store,
Till I mark'd the shaded gleaming
Of the sky, and yearn'd for more.

Eagerly the branches tearing,
Clear'd I all the space above,
Till the bolder gaze, high faring,
Scann'd the naked skies of Jove[1];
Deeps unguess'd now shone before me,
Splendid beam'd the solar car;
Wings of fervid fancy bore me
Out beyond the farthest star.

Reaching, gasping, wishing, longing
For the pageant brought to sight,
Vain I watch'd the gold orbs thronging

---

1. Jove: 罗马神话中主神朱庇特的别名。

那里色彩斑斓的树荫深处，
使我狂喜的麻醉般的咒法
来自绿草、蕨类还有花簇，
罂粟、夹竹桃以及繁缕花，
我躺卧良久，痴迷并幻想，
为自然慷慨的贮藏而欢乐，
直到我认出了遮住的亮光
来自天空，并且索求更多。

怀着急迫将枝条撕扯一空，
我将上方的空间彻底清除，
直到大胆的视线高高移行，
扫视着朱庇特赤裸的天幕；
未知的深渊在我面前展开，
日轮之光灿烂华美地倾泻；
洋溢幻象的羽翼将我承载
并把最最遥远的星辰穿越。

希冀，奢望，期盼，渴求
我目光中出现的宏伟盛景，
我徒劳望着那群金色星球

Round the celestial poles of light.
Madly on a moonbeam ladder
Heav'ns abyss I sought to scale,
Ever wiser, ever sadder,
As the fruitless task would fail.

Then, with futile striving sated,
Veer'd my soul to earth again,
Well content that I was fated
For a fair, yet low domain;
Pleasing thoughts of glad tomorrows,
Like the blissful moments past,
Lull'd to rest my transient sorrows,
Still'd my godless greed at last.

But my downward glance, returning,
Shrank in fright from what it spy'd;
Slopes in hideous torment burning,
Terror in the brooklet's tide:
For the dell, of shade denuded
By my desecrating hand,

围绕天际光明的极点转动。
疯狂地高踞在月光的阶梯
是我试图攀登的天国深渊，
智慧在增益，悲凄在加剧，
当那无果的任务最终枉然。

随后，厌倦了无功的追寻，
我的灵魂再度向地面回归，
心满意足于我注定的命运
当中那美丽而低下的范围；
愉快的思绪中欢畅的明日，
如同已经逝去的至福时刻，
安抚平复了我短暂的忧思，
最终将我渎神的贪欲缓和。

但我下视的目光，自归还，
就为瞥见的事物瑟瑟发抖；
山坡在骇人的苦痛中点燃，
恐怖充斥着小溪中的激流：
那座山谷，暴露在阴影里
只因为我双手的亵渎之故，

'Neath the bare sky blaz'd and brooded
As a lost, accursed land.

146
揭示

在裸露天空下燃烧并忧虑

成为一片失落受诅的废土。

屋宅
The House

　　发表于 1919 年 12 月 11 日的《国家询问报》。本诗与小说《畏避之屋》的灵感来源都是普罗维登斯市邦尼菲特街135 号的一栋老房子。

'Tis a grove-circled dwelling

Set close to a hill,

Where the branches are telling

Strange legends of ill;

Over timbers so old

That they breathe of the dead,

Crawl the vines, green and cold,

By strange nourishment fed;

And no man knows the juices they suck from the
  depths of their dank slimy bed.

In the gardens are growing

Tall blossoms and fair,

Each pallid bloom throwing

Perfume on the air;

But the afternoon sun

With its shining red rays

Makes the picture loom dun

On the curious gaze,

这坟墓环绕的住处

矗立在山丘的一侧，

那里的枝条在讲述

诡异而病态的传说；

蜿蜒在苍老的树干

使其如垂死般喘息，

那青翠寒冷的藤蔓，

将怪异的养分汲取；

无人知晓它们从阴暗湿滑的卧床深处

　　将何种汁液吮吸。．

在花园的里面长有

修长又美丽的鲜花，

苍白的花朵们任由

芳香在空气中飘洒；

只是那午后的烈日

用闪耀的红色光芒

将灰暗浮现的景致

映入了好奇的张望，

And above the sweet scent of the blossoms rise odours
of numberless days.

The rank grasses are waving
On terrace and lawn,
Dim memories savouring
Of things that have gone;
The stones of the walks
Are encrusted and wet,
And a strange spirit stalks
When the red sun has set.
And the soul of the watcher is fill'd with faint pictures
he fain would forget.

It was in the hot Junetime
I stood by that scene,
When the gold rays of noontime
Beat bright on the green.
But I shiver'd with cold,
Groping feebly for light,
As a picture unroll'd—
And my age-spanning sight
Saw the time I had been there before flash like fulgury
out of the night.

而不可计数的岁月的腐臭升起在花朵甜蜜的芬芳之上。

疯长而扭动的绿茵

将草地与阳台覆盖,

依稀的记忆在重温

那早已逝去的存在;

人行道上面的石料

已结满土垢并潮湿,

当陌生的灵体蹑脚

隐入红日西沉之时。

目击者的灵魂被他心中本想要忘却的微弱景象所充斥。

在酷热的六月之内

我来到此景前驻足,

当正午金色的光辉

在绿叶间闪耀夺目。

但我因寒冷而抖动,

无力地将光明搜掠,

当影像赫然间充盈——

我跨越时光的视野

看到了自己曾经来时的一幕闪现得如同电光划破黑夜。

城镇
The City

发表于《漂泊者》1919 年十月刊。

It was golden and splendid,

That City of light;

A vision suspended

In deeps of the night;

A region of wonder and glory, whose temples were

　　marble and white.

I remember the season

It dawn'd on my gaze;

The mad time of unreason,

The brain-numbing days

When Winter, white-sheeted and ghastly, stalks

　　onward to torture and craze.

More lovely than Zion [1]

It shone in the sky,

When the beams of Orion

Beclouded my eye,

---

1. Zion: 锡安, 耶路撒冷南部的圣山, 相传为耶和华居住之所。
这个名字也用于指代耶路撒冷全城和以色列全境。

何等金碧而辉煌，

那座光明的城镇；

一幕高悬的幻象

显露于夜的深沉；

那奇迹与光荣之地，洁白的大理石筑成的寺院成群。

仍记得那个时季

它闯入我的窥测；

那疯狂愚妄之际，

那大脑麻木之刻

当冬日，通体苍白而可怖，向前悄悄走入苦难与狂热。

可爱更甚于锡安

它在天空中亮起，

当猎户座的光线

将我的眼睛遮蔽，

Bringing sleep that was filled with dim mem'ries of
    moments obscure and gone by.

Its mansions were stately
With carvings made fair,
Each rising sedately
On terraces rare,
And the gardens were fragrant and bright with strange
    miracles blossoming there.

The avenues lur'd me
With vistas sublime;
Tall arches assur'd me
That once on a time
I had wander'd in rapture beneath them, and bask'd
    in the Halcyon clime.

On the plazas were standing
A sculptur'd array;
Long bearded, commanding,
Grave men in their day—
But one stood dismantled and broken, its bearded
    face battered away.

带来的睡梦充斥着模糊而消逝的时刻的朦胧记忆。

它的宏伟的建筑

有着美丽的雕廊，

各自平静地高矗

在珍奇的平台上，

而花园因那里盛开的奇异的魔法而变得芬芳明亮。

吸引着我的街道

有着非凡的景观；

飞拱们向我确保

在很久很久之前

我曾欣喜地漫步在它们下方，在宁静的气候中取暖。

在广场上面站定

一条雕像的长列；

长须，发号施令，

各自时代的人杰——

但其中一位支离破碎地伫立，长髯的面庞已经崩裂。

In that city effulgent
No mortal I saw,
But my fancy, indulgent
To memory's law,
Linger'd long on the forms in the plazas, and eyed their
  stone features with awe.

I fann'd the faint ember
That glow'd in my mind,
And strove to remember
The aeons behind;
To rove thro' infinity freely, and visit the past unconfin'd.

Then the horrible warning
Upon my soul sped
Like the ominous morning
That rises in red,
And in panic I flew from the knowledge of terrors
  forgotten and dead.

在这光辉的城里

我没有看到人类，

但我所想，姑息

于那记忆的法规，

惦念着广场上的塑像，凝望石质的面容时满怀敬畏。

我煽动微弱余火

使其在脑中旺炽，

并竭力想要记得

落在脑后的永世；

以自由漂泊着穿过无穷，并造访那毫无约束的往日。

随后可怖的警告

将我的灵魂催促

如同清晨的预兆

在血红当中跃出，

而我惊慌失措地逃离了获悉的遗忘而致命的恐怖。

致爱德华·约翰·莫顿·德
拉克斯·普伦基特，邓萨尼
男爵十八世
To Edward John Moreton Drax
Plunkett, Eighteenth Baron
Dunsany

发表于《试验》1919年十一月刊。爱德华·约翰·莫顿·
德拉克斯·普伦基特（1878—1957），英国 - 爱尔兰作家、
戏剧家，奇幻文学史上的重要人物，第十八世邓萨尼男爵。
邓萨尼本人在看过此诗后表示"精彩绝伦"以及"我非常感
谢作者在这首诗中韵律分明的温暖、慷慨的热情"。

As when the sun above a dusky wold,

Springs into sight and turns the gloom to gold,

Lights with his magic beams the dew-deck'd bow'r,

And wakes to life the gay responsive flow'r;

So now o'er realms where dark'ning dulness lies,

In solar state see shining **Plunkett** rise!

Monarch of Fancy! Whose ethereal mind

Mounts fairy peaks, and leaves the throng behind;

Whose soul untainted bursts the bounds of space,

And leads to regions of supernal grace:

Can any praise thee with too strong a tone,

Who in this age of folly gleam'd alone?

Thy quill, Dunsany, with an art divine

Recalls the gods to each deserted shrine;

From mystic air a novel pantheon makes,

And with new spirits fills the meads and brakes;

With thee we wander thro' primeval bow'rs,

164

致爱德华·约翰·莫顿·德拉克斯·普伦基特，邓萨尼男爵十八世

当那轮昏暗的荒原之上的太阳，

凸显于视野并将幽暗变成金黄，

魔力之光照亮缀满露水的树丛，

并将积极回应的花朵重新唤醒；

此刻在那暗色萧疏覆盖的领地，

闪耀的**普伦基特**在日出中升起！

幻想的君王！他超逸绝伦的念头

登上美的顶峰，将众人留在身后；

他纯洁的心灵冲破空间的拘束，

带领人走向神圣而优雅的国度：

人们怎么可能过分地将你赞美，

当你在这愚蠢的时代独自生辉？

你的妙笔，邓萨尼，用艺术的神圣

将神灵召回到荒弃的神龛当中；

从神秘的空气中造出虚幻诸神，

并在草地和树丛布满新的精魂；

我们随你在原始的树荫下流连，

For thou hast brought earth's childhood back, and ours!
How leaps the soul, with sudden bliss increas'd,
When led by thee to lands beyond the East!
Sick of this sphere, in crime and conflict old,
We yearn for wonders distant and untold;
O'er Homer's page a second time we pore,
And rack our brains for gleams of infant lore:
But all in vain—for valiant tho' we strive
No common means these pictures can revive.
*Then dawns **Dunsany** with celestial light*
And fulgent visions break upon our sight:
His barque enchanted each sad spirit bears
To shores of gold, beyond the reach of cares.
No earthly trammels now our thoughts may chain;
For childhood's fancy hath come back again!
What glitt'ring worlds now wait our eager eyes!
What roads untrodden beckon thro' the skies!
Wonders on wonders line the gorgeous ways,
And glorious vistas greet the ravish'd gaze;
Mountains of clouds, castles of crystal dreams,
Ethereal cities and Elysian streams;

166

因为你带回大地与我们的童年！

灵魂不住欢跃，并瞬间生出至福，

当被你引领至东方更远的乐土！

厌倦了这颗行星，罪恶冲突已久，

我们将未讲述的遥远奇迹渴求；

我们重新开始钻研荷马的篇章，

并绞尽脑汁寻求童年记忆之光：

但只是徒劳——虽然我们锐意拼争

通常的办法不能复原那些图景。

然后**邓萨尼**随着天光渐渐浮现

瑰丽的幻影显露于我们的视线：

他醉人的轻舟承载悲伤的灵魂

前往黄金海岸，令忧愁不可接近。

世事桎梏再难禁锢我们的思维；

因为童年的想象已经再度回归！

何等辉煌的世界守候渴望之眼！

何等光洁的道路越过天空呼唤！

无数的奇观行进于华美的道路，

壮丽的景色迎接着入迷的瞩目；

云朵的山脉，晶莹的梦境的堡垒，

缥缈的城市以及天国般的溪水；

Temples of blue, where myriad stars adore

Forgotten gods of aeons gone before!

Such are thine arts, **Dunsany**, such thy skill,

That scarce terrestrial seems thy moving quill;

Can man, and man alone, successful draw

Such scenes of wonder and domains of awe?

Our hearts, enraptur'd, fix thy mind's abode

In high Pegāna[1] : hail thee as a god;

And sure, can aught more high or godlike be

Than such a fancy as resides in thee?

Delighted Pan[2] a friend and peer perceives

As thy sweet music stirs the sylvan leaves;

The Nine[3], transported, bless thy golden lyre:

Approve thy fancy, and applaud thy fire;

Whilst Jove himself assumes a brother's tone,

And vows thy pantheon equal to his own.

Dunsany, may thy days be glad and long;

Replete with visions, and atune with song;

May thy rare notes increasing millions cheer,

---

1. Pegāna: 佩迦纳，邓萨尼虚构的白色群山，每一座山顶都有一位神灵。《佩迦纳诸神》是邓萨尼出版的第一部作品，也是其代表作之一。

2. Pan: 潘神，希腊神话中半人半羊的森林之神。

3. The Nine: 九神，埃及神话中拉、舒、泰芙努特、盖布、努特、奥西里斯、伊西斯、塞特、奈芙蒂斯九位神灵的总称。

致爱德华·约翰·莫顿·德拉克斯·普伦基特，邓萨尼男爵十八世。

蔚蓝的庙宇上，无数的繁星拜祭

消逝的万古之中被遗忘的神祇！

你的艺术如是，**邓萨尼**，这等技巧，

使你飞扬的妙笔显得超出地表；

仅靠人自身怎可能成功地描绘

如此奇妙的景象与惊人的范围？

我们的心，狂喜着，投向你心所在

崇高的佩迦纳：将你如神明崇拜；

是啊，有什么更加崇高或是神奇

与你内心之中这般的想象相比？

快乐的潘神看到了友人与同伴

当你甜美的音乐撼动林间叶片；

九神，欣喜若狂，赐予你黄金诗琴：

赞许你的幻想，并夸奖你的热忱；

朱庇特本尊也如兄长般的发话，

宣布你的万神殿与祂那座等价。

邓萨尼，愿你的岁月快乐而悠长；

被幻影所充满，并有着歌曲飘扬；

愿你珍贵的笔录多多激励万众，

Thy name beloved, and thy mem'ry dear!

'Tis thou who hast in hours of dulness brought

New charms of language, and new gems of thought;

Hast with a poet's grace enrich'd the earth

With aureate dreams as noble as thy birth.

Grateful we name thee, bright with fix'd renown,

The fairest jewel in Hibernia's [1] crown.

---

1. Hibernia: 海伯尼亚，爱尔兰岛的古典拉丁文名称。

致爱德华·约翰·莫顿·德拉克斯·普伦基特，邓萨尼男爵十八世。

你的名字被爱，你的记忆被珍重！
是你在那些黯淡的时刻中带去
语言新的魅力，以及思想的珠玉；
并带着诗人的优雅装饰了地面
用你所生出的华丽的金色梦幻。
我们感激地称呼你，光辉的名士，
海伯尼亚的王冠上最美的宝石。

To Edward John Moreton Drax Plunkett, Eighteenth Baron Dunsany

钟声
Bells

发表于《试验》1919 年十二月刊。

I hear the bells from yon imposing tow'r;
The bells of Yuletide o'er a troubled night;
Pealing with mock'ry in a dismal hour
Upon a world upheav'd greed and fright.

Their mellow tones on myriad roofs resound;
A million restless souls attend the chime;
Yet falls their message on a stony ground—
Their spirit slaughter'd with the sword of Time.

Why ring in counterfeit of happy years
When calm and quiet rul'd the placid plain?
Why with familiar strains arouse the tears
Of those who ne'er may know content again?

How well I knew ye once—so long ago—
When slept the ancient village on the slope;
Then rang your accents o'er the starlit snow
In gladness, peace, and sempiternal hope.

174

钟声

我听到钟声传出自雄伟的塔楼；

那些圣诞之钟穿过忧郁的黑夜；

满怀着讥讽在阴沉的时刻鼓奏

飘散在崛起的贪婪恐怖的世界。

圆润的音调在无数屋顶上萦回；

令万千个无眠的灵魂悉心听闻；

它们的讯息却向石质地面下坠——

时间的利刃屠尽了它们的心神。

为何这长鸣假扮出欢欣的年华

当安宁的平原充满祥和与静谧？

为何迸发的泪水随熟悉的重压

在无缘再见此景之人眼中洋溢？

我曾经与你相熟——早在当初——

当古老的村庄熟睡在山坡之上；

你的声音在星光下的雪地散布

充满欢乐、安详，和永恒的希望。

175

Bells

In fancy yet I view the modest spire;
The peaked roof, cast dark against the moon;
The Gothic windows, glowing with a fire
That lent enchantment to the brazen tune.

Lovely each snow-drap'd hedge beneath the beams
That added silver to the silver there;
Graceful each col, each lane, and all the streams,
And glad the spirit of the pine-ting'd air.

A simple creed the rural swains profess'd,
In simple bliss among the hills they dwelt;
Their hearts were light, their honest souls at rest;
Cheer'd with the joys by reas'ning mortals felt.

But on the scene a hideous blight intrudes;
A lurid nimbus hovers o'er the land;
Demoniac shades low'r black above the woods,
And by each door malignant shadows stand.

想象之中我又看到庄重的塔尖；

升起的屋檐，向月亮投去阴影；

哥特式的窗棂，熊熊燃起火焰

将魔力注入了黄铜的音调当中。

月光之下积雪覆盖的可爱树篱

将银白色的景致更添一层银白；

幽雅的山口、巷陌与每条小溪，

心灵因松香浸染的空气无比愉快。

村里的农夫信奉的简单的准则，

是他们居住的山中简单的至福；

他们内心光明，心灵诚恳平和；

由于理性带来的喜悦欢欣鼓舞。

但可怖的灾祸侵入了这幕景象；

整片土地上盘旋着骇人的雨云；

着魔的影迹在林梢漆黑地沉降，

恶毒的阴翳伫立在每一座大门。

The jester Time stalks darkly thro' the mead;
Beneath his tread contentment dies away.
Hearts that were light with causeless anguish bleed,
And restless soul proclaims his evil sway.

Conflict and change beset the tott'ring world;
Wild thoughts and fancies fill the common mind;
Confusion on a senile race is hurl'd,
And crime and folly wander unconfin'd.

I heard the bells—the mocking, cursed bells
That wake dim memories to haunt and chill;
Ringing and ringing o'er a thousand hells—
Fiends of the Night—why can ye not be still?

时间这名小丑暗暗将草地穿越；

在它的脚步之下满足从此消逝。

曾经光明的心无端因剧痛流血，

无眠的灵魂显出它邪恶的统治。

矛盾与变迁困扰着飘摇的世间，

妄念和幻影充斥了平凡的脑海；

衰老的种族之中被掷入了混乱，

罪恶与痴愚在无拘无束地徘徊。

我听到钟声——受诅的嘲讽钟声

萦绕并恐吓着醒来的模糊记忆；

在一千层地狱上不断发出长鸣——

黑夜的魔鬼——为何你不肯平息？

梦魇之湖
The Nightmare Lake

发表于《漂泊者》1919 年十二月刊。这首诗所描写的景象成为沉没于哈利湖底的卡尔克萨城的灵感来源。

There is a lake in distant Zan [1] *,*

Beyond the wonted haunts of man,

Where broods alone in a hideous state

A spirit dead and desolate;

A spirit ancient and unholy,

Heavy with fearsome melancholy,

Which from the waters dull and dense

Draws vapors cursed with pestilence.

Around the banks, a mire of clay,

Sprawl things offensive in decay,

And curious birds that reach that shore

Are seen by mortals nevermore.

Here shines by day the searing sun

On glassy wastes beheld by none,

And here by night pale moonbeams flow

Into the deeps that yawn below.

In nightmares only is it told

What scenes beneath those beams unfold;

---

1. Zan: 赞恩，虚构地点，其具体位置不明。

在遥远的赞恩有一面湖水，

隔绝于尘世间人迹的萦回，

在那里可怖地独自沉思着

一个死去而又悲哀的魂魄；

这个古老而又不洁的灵体，

满载着忧愁从而令人畏惧，

它使稠密无光的水体之中

被疫病所诅咒的迷雾升腾。

湖岸之旁，一处黏土泥潭，

将衰败中的恶意之物蔓延，

而抵达了湖畔的好奇之鸟

从此再也不会被人们看到。

这里的白昼有毒辣的日头

照向无人注目的沉闷荒丘，

这里的黑夜有苍白的月光

向着下界裂开的深渊流淌。

只有在梦魇当中才能得知

何样的景象会在月下揭示；

What scenes, too old for human sight,

Lie sunken there in endless night;

For in those depths there only pace

The shadows of a voiceless race.

One midnight, redolent of ill,

I saw that lake, asleep and still;

While in the lurid sky there rode

A gibbous moon that glow'd and glow'd.

I saw the stretching marshy shore,

And the foul things those marshes bore:

Lizards and snakes convuls'd and dying;

Ravens and vampires putrefying;

All these, and hov'ring o'er the dead,

Narcophagi that on them fed.

And as the dreadful moon climb'd high,

Fright'ning the stars from out the sky,

I saw the lake's dull water glow

Till sunken things appear'd below.

There shone unnumber'd fathoms down,

The tow'rs of a forgotten town;

The tarnish'd domes and mossy walls;

那些景象苍老得无法辨别，

静静在此沉入无尽的长夜；

而在深渊之中徘徊的仅剩

某个无声眷族的成群黑影。

一个充满病态的午夜时刻，

我看到那平静沉睡的湖泊；

而漂浮在骇人的夜空之内

一轮凸月正不断放出光辉。

我看到岸边泥泞向外伸出，

泥泞中诞生出了肮脏之物：

蜥蜴与蛇群在垂死地痉挛；

渡鸦与吸血蝙蝠全身腐烂；

除此外，还有盘踞于尸体，

食腐的恶灵正在大快朵颐。

随着阴森的孤月高高上升，

使得天外的星辰感到惊恐，

我看到湖中死水映着光芒

直到沉没的事物穷形尽相。

闪耀在数不尽的深度之下，

是座遗忘之城的林立高塔；

有着苔痕之墙和暗色穹顶；

Weed-tangled spires and empty halls;
Deserted fanes and vaults of dread,
And streets of gold uncoveted.
These I beheld, and saw beside
A horde of shapeless shadows glide;
A noxious horde which to my glance
Seem'd moving in a hideous dance
Round slimy sepulchres that lay
Beside a never-travell'd way.
Straight from those tombs a heaving rose
That vex'd the waters' dull repose,
While lethal shades of upper space
Howl'd at the moon's sardonic face.
Then sank the lake within its bed,
Suck'd down to caverns of the dead,
Till from the reeking, new-stript earth
Curl'd foetid fumes of noisome birth.
About the city, nigh uncover'd,
The monstrous dancing shadows hover'd,
When lo! There oped with sudden stir
The portal of each sepulchre!

水草间的塔楼和无人大厅；
荒弃的寺院与可怕的墓穴，
与无瑕的黄金筑成的长街。
除了目睹这些，我还看见
一群形态不定的黑影盘桓；
这可憎的群体正如我看到
似乎跳起某种丑恶的舞蹈
它们所环绕的浸水的坟墓
紧邻一条无人涉足的道路。
坟墓前方有一座土丘高耸
扰乱了湖水中沉闷的宁静，
而致命的阴影们置身高处
向着月亮嘲弄的脸庞狂呼。
最后那片湖在河床中下沉，
被死者们的洞穴一饮而尽，
直到恶臭中，崭露的土壤
将污秽而新生的臭气飘扬。
而那座城市，快露出水面，
畸形舞动的阴影绕城盘旋，
快看！突然间的一阵摇摆
使每一座坟墓的入口敞开！

No ear may learn, no tongue may tell
What nameless horror then befell.
I see that lake—that moon agrin—
That city and the things within—
Waking, I pray that on that shore
The nightmare lake may sink no more!

耳边辨不清，口中道不明

会有何种无名的恐怖发生。

我看到湖泊——月亮在冷笑——

那座城市将种种存在围绕——

醒来后，我祈祷彼岸之旁

梦魇之湖永远不要再下降！

读邓萨尼勋爵《奇迹之书》有感
On Reading Lord Dunsany's Book of Wonder

发表于《银号角》1920 年三月刊。《奇迹之书》是邓萨尼在 1912 年出版的短篇小说集。

The hours of night unheeded fly,
And in the grate the embers fade;
Vast shadows one by one pass by
In silent daemon cavalcade.

But still the magic volume holds
The raptur'd eye in realms apart,
And fulgent sorcery enfolds
The willing mind and eager heart.

The lonely room no more is there—
For to the sight in pomp appear
Temples and cities pois'd in air
And blazing glories—sphere on sphere.

读邓萨尼勋爵《奇迹之书》有感

夜晚的时光无形间飞过，
炉栅中的余烬渐渐熄灭；
巨大的影迹依次地穿梭
汇入沉默的精灵的行列。

但奇妙的书卷仍然束缚
狂喜之眼于遥远的疆域，
而光芒四射的法术揽入
渴望的心与热切的思绪。

孤寂的房间已离开原位——
宏伟的景象浮现在眼前
庙宇和城市在空中准备
并放出光彩——一环又一环。

致梦中人
To a Dreamer

发表于《草原狼》1921 年一月刊。洛夫克拉夫特在给弗兰克·贝尔纳普·朗的一封信中提及，这首诗的灵感产生于阅读法国诗人波德莱尔的笔记。

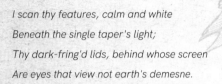

I scan thy features, calm and white
Beneath the single taper's light;
Thy dark-fring'd lids, behind whose screen
Are eyes that view not earth's demesne.

And as I look, I fain would know
The paths whereon thy dream-steps go;
The spectral realms that thou canst see
With eyes veil'd from the world and me.

For I have likewise gaz'd in sleep
On things my mem'ry scarce can keep,
And from half-knowing long to spy
Again the scenes before thine eye.

196
致梦中人

我眼中你的面容，苍白平静地
笼罩于一盏光芒微弱的烛火；
那黑暗下的眼帘，在其后藏有
一双观望着地外空间的眼眸。

在我端详时，我多么渴望知晓
幻梦的脚步会踏上哪条轨道；
你将要看到的影影绰绰的异域
来自与尘世和我隔绝的眼底。

因为我也曾一样在睡梦中注目
那些记忆所难以留存的事物，
而仅存的知觉使我期待着窥视
在你的眼前再度浮现的景致。

I, too, have known the peaks of Thok [1] ;
The vales of Pnath [2] , where dream-shapes flock;
The vaults of Zin [3] —and well I trow
Why thou demand'st that taper's glow.

But what is this that subtly slips
Over thy face and bearded lips?
What fear distracts thy mind and heart,
That drops must from thy forehead start?

Old visions wake—thine op'ning eyes
Gleam black with clouds of other skies,
And as from some demoniac sight
I flee into the haunted night.

---

1. Thok: 索克，黑暗行星犹格斯的双子卫星之一。

2. vales of Pnath: 纳斯峡谷，幻梦境中的地底深渊，充满堆积如山的白骨。巨噬蠕虫们在此栖息，夜魇也经常将猎物带到此地任其死亡。

3. vaults of Zin: 辛之墓室，幻梦境中的庞大洞窟，古革巨人和妖鬼的栖息地。

致梦中人

我也曾一样知悉了索克的山峰；

梦境生物在纳斯峡谷中群行；

以及辛之墓室——但我不了解

你为何需要这盏烛火的摇曳。

而又是什么东西正微妙地套紧

你的脸庞和生有髭须的嘴唇？

是何种会令人心神不宁的惊吓，

使汗珠开始从你的前额下滑？

旧日之影觉醒——你双眼睁开

映出多云的异界天空的阴霾，

而感受到了彼端魔鬼般的视线

我逃入了那鬼影幢幢的夜晚。

题于一本王尔德童话集
With a Copy of Wilde's Fairy Tales

　　创作于 1920 年 7 月。这首诗是诗人给爱丽丝 · M. 哈姆雷特的赠诗，这位志同道合的伙伴将邓萨尼的作品推荐给了洛夫克拉夫特。奥斯卡 · 王尔德（1854—1900），爱尔兰作家、诗人、剧作家，英国唯美主义艺术运动的倡导者。

Madam, in whom benignant gods have join'd
The gifts of fancy, melody, and mind;
Whose kindly guidance first enrich'd my sight
With great DUNSANY'S Heliconian light:
Pray take from one so deeply in thy debt
These jewell'd thoughts, by master artist set;
For sure (except for PLUNKETT'S dreams alone)
The dreams of Wilde are nearest to thine own.
Here wilt thou find, in pleasing order fix'd,
A host of golden fantasies unmix'd;
Tales that the dust of modern life dispel,
And take us back to fairyland to dwell.
May each quaint story, told with magic pow'r,
Speed the still moments of some leisure hour;
To rural shades a keener beauty add,
Or help to make thy winter fireside glad.
Yet slight indeed the trivial gift must seem,
If measur'd by the giver's firm esteem!

题于一本王尔德童话集

女士，仁慈的诸神在你身上注入

幻想、旋律以及心灵的过人天赋；

你亲切的指引曾使我眼界大开

映入邓萨尼的赫利孔式的光彩。

请从对你深深感激之人手中接过

这些珠玉之论，被艺术大师创作；

无疑（除了普伦基特的梦境本身）

来自王尔德的幻梦与你最为贴近。

你会发现其中，美妙有序地珍藏

为数众多、纯洁无瑕的金色狂想；

这些传说将现代生活的尘俗抹去，

带领我们回到童话王国之中安居。

愿每个老故事，都以其中的魔法，

拨快这段平静时光中的些许闲暇；

在乡村的阴霾中增添期待的美妙，

或是在你冬日的炉火旁带来欢笑。

这份微薄的赠礼似乎的确太轻，

若是相比于赠予者真诚的尊重！

With a Copy of Wilde's Fairy Tales

读哈珀·威廉姆斯《林中怪物》

[On The Thing in the Woods by Harper Williams]

出自洛夫克拉夫特在 1924 年 11 月写给莉莉安·D. 克拉克的一封信，作者在信中声称，本诗是他题于《林中怪物》扉页，给弗兰克·贝尔纳普·朗的赠诗。哈珀·威廉姆斯是英国-美国童话作家玛格丽·威廉姆斯（1881—1944）的笔名，恐怖小说《林中怪物》出版于 1913 年，并于 1924 年再版。

BELKNAP, accept from Theobald's spectral Claw
These haunting Chapters of daemoniack Awe;
Such nightmare Yarns we both have often writ,
With goblin Whispers, and an Hint of IT,
Till sure, we're like to think all Terror's grown
A sort of private Product of our own!
Lest, then, our Pride our sober Sense mislead,
And make us copyright each hellish Deed,
'Tis ours to see what ghastly Flames can blaze
From Spooks and Ghouls that other Wizards raise!

206

读哈珀·威廉姆斯《林中怪物》

贝尔纳普，请从西奥伯德的魔爪中收下

这些难以忘却的章节，像恶魔一样可怕；

这种噩梦般的故事我们两人经常创作，

充满地精的低语，以及那东西的线索，

未及确认，但我们都觉得这些恐怖生出

属于我们自己的某一种私有产物！

那么为防我们被自矜和冷静的意识欺骗，

试图去取得每个地狱中契约的版权，

让我们看看何等可怖的烈焰会熠熠生辉

于其他巫师召唤的幽灵与食尸鬼！

猫
The Cats

创作于 1925 年 2 月。洛夫克拉夫特喜欢猫，并且养有一只名叫"小黑"的猫。

Babels of blocks to the high heavens tow'ring,
  Flames of futility swirling below;
Poisonous fungi in brick and stone flow'ring,
  Lanterns that shudder and death-lights that glow.

Black monstrous bridges across oily rivers,
  Cobwebs of cable by nameless things spun;
Catacomb deeps whose dank chaos delivers
  Streams of live foetor, that rots in the sun.

Colour and splendour, disease and decaying,
  Shrieking and ringing and scrambling insane,
Rabbles exotic to stranger-gods praying,
  Jumbles of odour that stifle the brain.

Legions of cats from the alleys nocturnal,
  Howling and lean in the glare of the moon,
Screaming the future with mouthings infernal,
  Yelling the burden of Pluto's red rune.

石块砌成的高塔耸立直入天空，

　　无足挂齿的火舌在下方旋转；

剧毒的真菌在砖石间生长旺盛，

　　颤抖的灯笼将死亡之光闪现。

可怖的黑色桥梁跨过油污之河，

　　交错的缆绳被无名之物缠拽；

阴湿混沌的墓穴深渊中淌出的

　　恶臭的溪流，在阳光下腐坏。

光彩伴着盛景，疫病偕同腐朽，

　　尖叫、鸣响，在疯狂中相抵，

异乡群氓向着陌生的神灵祈求，

　　杂乱汇聚的臭气使大脑窒息。

一大群猫儿置身于夜间的小巷，

　　在刺眼的月光之下嚎叫蜷伏，

用地狱般的口齿向着未来叫嚷，

　　负担着冥王星的赤印并高呼。

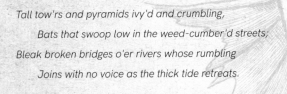

Tall tow'rs and pyramids ivy'd and crumbling,
  Bats that swoop low in the weed-cumber'd streets;
Bleak broken bridges o'er rivers whose rumbling
  Joins with no voice as the thick tide retreats.

Belfries that blackly against the moon totter,
  Caverns whose mouths are by mosses effac'd,
And living to answer the wind and the water,
  Only the lean cats that howl in the waste!

猫

高台和金字塔在青藤下面坍塌，

　　蝙蝠在杂草丛生的街头翻飞；

河流的低鸣从阴郁的断桥之下

　　无声地汇入退去的宏大潮水。

钟楼昏昏沉沉紧倚着月光跛行，

　　洞穴的巨口被重重青苔抹消，

存活并回应着风与水流的生命，

　　仅有荒野中嚎叫的瘦弱的猫！

春
Primavera

发表于《布鲁克林人》1925 年四月刊。

There is wonder on land and billow,
    And a strangeness in bough and vein,
For the brook or the budded willow
    Feel the Presence walking again.
It has come in the olden fashion,
    As the tritest of lutes have sung,
But it carries the olden passion
    That can never be aught but young.

There are whispers from groves auroral
    To blood half-afraid to hear,
While the evening star's faint choral
    Is an ecstasy touch'd with fear.
And at night where the hill-wraiths rally
    Glows the far Walpurgis[1] flame,
Which the lonely swain in the valley
    Beholds, tho' he dare not name.

---

1. Walpurgis: 瓦尔普吉斯，中欧与北欧地区的节日，其主题
通常为"迎接春天"与"女巫之夜"。相传在瓦尔普吉斯之夜，
女巫们会从四面八方赶赴哈尔茨山的布罗肯峰，举行盛大的仪
式并燃起熊熊篝火。

216
春

奇迹正出现于泥土与气流，

　　新奇感充斥着枝条与叶脉，

因为小溪以及发芽的新柳

　　感受到那再度降临的存在。

它在古老的装束之下现身，

　　和陈旧的诗琴传唱中一样，

但它所带来的古老的热忱

　　将永远不会褪尽它的韶光。

低语声传出自破晓的林中

　　令聆听的血裔们感到惊悸，

黄昏之星发出的微弱和声

　　有如被恐惧所染指的狂喜。

夜晚山间恶灵们集会之处

　　远远点燃瓦尔普吉斯之火，

而置身于山谷的孤单农夫

　　亲眼见证，却不敢于言说。

Primavera

And in every wild breeze falling
   Out of spaces beyond the sky,
There are ancient voices calling
   To regions remote and high;
To the gardens of elfin glory
   That lie o'er the purple seas,
And mansions of dream and story
   From childhood memories.

I am call'd where the still dawns glitter
   On pastures and furrow'd crests,
And the thrush and the wood-lark twitter
   Low over their brookside nests;
Where the smoke of the cottage hovers,
   And the elm-buds promise their shade,
And a carpet of new green covers
   The floor of the forest glade.

I am call'd where the vales are dreaming
   In golden, celestial light,
With the gables of castles gleaming,

随着每一阵风狂野地飘散

　　超出了天空并将宇宙穿越，
远古的声音所发出的呼唤

　　飘扬在遥远并崇高的异界；
飘扬在小巧而美丽的花圃

　　此地高悬于那紫色的海水，
而装满梦想和故事的别墅

　　来自童年生活的记忆之内。

我被召唤之地有黎明闪耀

　　在牧场和沟壑密布的山巅，
鸫鸟和云雀交相发出鸣叫

　　它们在河岸的巢窠上低悬；
那里有炊烟从小屋中升起，

　　榆树的嫩芽们预示着阴凉，
而一层新绿色的绒毯遮蔽

　　在树林间空地的表层之上。

我被召唤之地有山谷入梦

　　于金黄色天光的笼罩之内，
那里城堡的外墙通体澄明，

And village roofs steep and bright;
With distant spires set slimly
Over tangles of twining boughs,
And a ribbon of river seen dimly
Thro' fields that the farmer ploughs.

I am call'd where a twilight ocean
Laps the piers of an ancient town,
And dream-ships in ghostly motion
Ride at anchor up and down;
Where sea-lanes narrow and bending
Climb steep thro' the fragrant gloom
Of chimneys and gambrels blending
With orchard branches in bloom.

And when o'er the waves enchanted
The moon and the stars appear,
I am haunted—haunted—haunted
By dreams of a mystic year;
Of a year long lost in the dawning,
When the planets were vague and pale,

村庄里的屋顶陡峭而生辉；

而远方的尖塔微弱地显露

在盘结扭曲的枝干的上侧，

丝带一般的河水渺渺忽忽

将农夫所耕耘的田地穿过。

我被召唤之地有暮光之海

拍打某座古老城镇的桥墩，

梦境之船的律动犹如鬼怪

将抛锚的动作一次次复循；

那里的海滨小巷狭窄扭曲

在幽香的黑暗中陡然升高

直至层叠密布的烟囱屋脊

以及果园之中盛开的枝条。

高高升起于沉醉中的海波

明月与漫天星辰一同显现，

我身边萦绕着——萦绕着——萦绕着

来自神秘年代之中的梦幻；

那个年代遗失于晨光已久，

那时候的行星苍白并模糊，

And the chasms of space were yawning
  To vistas that fade and fail.

I am haunted by recollections
  Of lands that were not of earth,
Of places where mad perfections
  In horror were brought to birth;
Where pylons of onyx mounted
  To heavens with fire embower'd,
And turrets and domes uncounted
  O'er the terrac'd torrents tower'd.

I am call'd to these reachless regions
  In tones that are old and known,
By a chorus of phantom legions
  That must have been once my own—
But the spell is a charm swift fleeting,
  And the earth has a potent thrall,
So I never have known the freeing,
  Or heeded the springtime's call.

而宇宙中的裂痕张开巨口

    向着消隐而又失落的景物。

我身边萦绕着的纷纷往事

    来自一方地球之外的异乡，

那个地方有着疯狂的极致

    在恐惧之中被诞生在世上；

那里有着玛瑙的塔架高耸

    直入火焰穹隆覆盖的天际，

而不可计数的塔楼与拱顶

    在阶梯状的激流上空林立。

从遥不可及之地召唤我的

    是那古老而又熟悉的乡音，

众多的幽魂们合唱的颂歌

    必然曾一度归属于我自身——

但那咒语的魔力很快飘走，

    而大地是一座严密的监牢，

所以我从来都不了解自由，

    也一直没有回应春的号召。

节日
Festival

发表于《诡丽奇谭》1926 年十二月刊。这首诗本是洛夫克拉夫特献给编辑法恩斯沃斯·莱特的圣诞诗歌，后者由于太过喜欢此诗将其刊登了出来，却删去了最后一段留给自己。

There is snow on the ground,

    And the valleys are cold,

And a midnight profound

    Blackly squats o'er the wold;

But a light on the hilltops half-seen hints of feastings

    unhallow'd and old.

There is death in the clouds,

    There is fear in the night,

For the dead in their shrouds

    Hail the sun's turning flight,

And chant wild in the woods as they dance round a

    Yule -altar[1] fungous and white.

---

1. Yule: 耶鲁节，古代日耳曼民族的宗教节日，庆祝主题据传为狂猎、奥丁大神或是盎格鲁 - 撒克逊异教中的夜间圣母。在基督教改造后逐渐演变成了今天的圣诞节。

地表覆盖着积雪，

    山谷充满了严寒，

深不可测的午夜

    沉沉蹲伏在荒原；

而山顶若隐若现的光芒暗示着不洁的古老盛筵。

死气深藏于云朵，

    夜晚已变得可怖，

裹尸布中的死者

    为太阳转向欢呼，

他们在林中生霉的白色耶鲁节祭坛边欢歌起舞。

To no gale of earth's kind
    Sways the forest of oak,
Where the sick boughs entwin'd
    By mad mistletoes [1] choke,
For these pow'rs are the pow'rs of the dark, from the graves of the
    lost Druid-folk.

And mayst thou to such deeds
    Be an abbot and priest,
Singing cannibal greeds
    At each devil-wrought feast,
And to all the incredulous world shewing dimly the sign of the beast.

---

1. mistletoe: 槲寄生，檀香目桑寄生科植物，在欧洲神话、传说与习俗中有重要含义，在现代社会作为圣诞节的装饰物与象征物使用。

来自地外的狂飙

在橡树森林吹袭，

病态的扭曲枝条

因疯槲寄生窒息。

这些黑暗的力量源自德鲁伊信徒失落的墓地。

愿君能有所成就

将修士牧者担当，

歌颂食人的欲求

在每个邪宴之上，

在这个疑虑重重的世间模糊地揭示野兽的迹象。

城郊的万圣夜
Hallowe'en in a Suburb

发表于《全国业余作家刊物》1926 年三月刊。

The steeples are white in the wild moonlight,

   And the trees have a silver glare;

Past the chimneys high see the vampires fly,

   And the harpies [1] of upper air,

   That flutter and laugh and stare.

For the village dead to the moon outspread

   Never shone in the sunset's gleam,

But grew out of the deep that the dead years keep

   Where the rivers of madness stream

   Down the gulfs to a pit of dream.

A chill wind weaves thro' the rows of sheaves

   In the meadows that shimmer pale,

And comes to twine where the headstones shine

   And the ghouls of the churchyard wail

   For harvests that fly and fail.

---

1. harpy: 鹰身女妖，又译哈比或哈耳庇厄，希腊神话中半人半鸟的生物，生性贪婪淫邪。

尖塔在荒凉的明月下通体皎洁，
　　　而树林将银色的光芒闪耀；
高峻的烟囱上空有吸血鬼飞行，
　　　以及上方更高处的鹰身女妖，
　　　在纷飞着投下目光和欢笑。

虽然蔓延的月光下垂死的村庄
　　　永远不会因熹微的落日亮起，
却超脱了沦入死亡岁月的渊谷
　　　那里的河水涌出疯狂之溪
　　　穿过海湾向着梦的深渊流去。

一阵凉风迂回穿过一捆捆麦穗
　　　四周的草场在黯淡地闪烁，
它转而盘旋在发亮的墓碑之间
　　　那片墓园的食尸鬼们哀号着
　　　痛惜飞走并遗失的收获。

Not a breath of the strange grey gods of change
        That tore from the past its own
Can quicken this hour, when a spectral pow'r
        Spreads deep o'er the cosmic throne
        And looses the vast unknown.

So here again stretch the vale and plain
        That moons long-forgotten saw,
And the dead leap gay in the pallid ray,
        Sprung out of the tomb's black maw
        To shake all the world with awe.

And all that the morn shall greet forlorn,
        The ugliness and the pest
Of rows where thick rise the stones and brick,
        Shall some day be with the rest,
        And brood with the shades unblest.

诡秘苍老的神主们变幻的吹拂
　　分割于其自身拥有的往日
却无法加速此际，当幽冥之力
　　在宇宙的王座上深邃地充斥
　　并释放出了巨大的未知。

而此处再度延展的谷地和平原
　　曾被久已遗忘的月光注目，
死者在苍白的光中欢快地跳动，
　　它们从坟墓黑暗的裂口涌出
　　意图使整个世界陷入恐怖。

晨光会以凄绝将这一切迎接，
　　那些丑恶之物以及害虫
的行列置身于砖石林立之地，
　　某一日将和余者们一同
　　随着诅咒的暗影大量滋生。

Then wild in the dark let the lemurs bark,
  And the leprous spires ascend;
For new and old alike in the fold
  Of horror and death are penn'd,
  For the hounds of Time to rend.

城郊的万圣夜

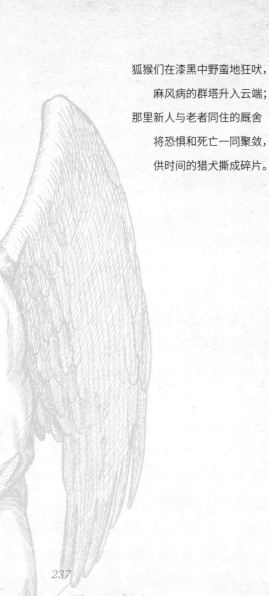

狐猴们在漆黑中野蛮地狂吠，
　　麻风病的群塔升入云端；
那里新人与老者同住的厩舍
　　将恐惧和死亡一同聚敛，
　　供时间的猎犬撕成碎片。

读安布罗斯·比尔斯
[On Ambrose Bierce]

出自洛夫克拉夫特在 1927 年 6 月写给弗兰克·贝尔纳普·朗的一封信。安布罗斯·比尔斯（1842—？），美国作家、记者、诗人，以恐怖的题材和辛辣的笔法著称，在参加墨西哥内战后下落不明。本诗反映了洛夫克拉夫特、朗与萨缪尔·洛夫曼关于比尔斯"绿色氛围效应"所产生效果的一段辩论：洛夫曼声称看见蓝色，朗则声称看见绿色。

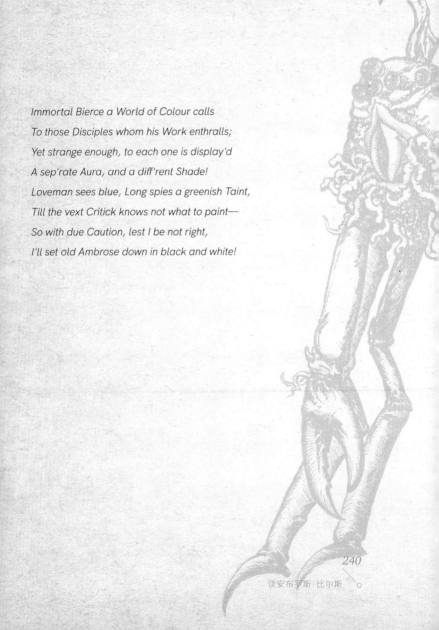

Immortal Bierce a World of Colour calls
To those Disciples whom his Work enthralls;
Yet strange enough, to each one is display'd
A sep'rate Aura, and a diff'rent Shade!
Loveman sees blue, Long spies a greenish Taint,
Till the vext Critick knows not what to paint—
So with due Caution, lest I be not right,
I'll set old Ambrose down in black and white!

240

不朽者比尔斯，多彩的世界在高呼
被他的杰作所迷倒的众位信徒；
异乎寻常，每个人的眼前都展开
独有的氛围，以及与众不同的色彩！
洛夫曼看见蓝，朗看见绿色的墨渍，
而烦恼的批评家对绘画一无所知——
怀着应有的谨慎，以防我犯下过错，
我会将老安布罗斯书写于黑白两色！

树林
The Wood

发表于《试验》1929 年一月刊。

They cut it down, and where the pitch-black aisles
        Of forest night had hid eternal things,
They scal'd the sky with tow'rs and marble piles
        To make a city for their revellings.

White and amazing to the lands around
        That wondrous wealth of domes and turrets rose;
Crystal and ivory, sublimely crown'd
        With pinnacles that bore unmelting snows.

And through its halls the pipe and sistrum[1] rang,
        While wine and riot brought their scarlet stains;
Never a voice of elder marvels sang,
        Nor any eye call'd up the hills and plains.

Thus down the years, till on one purple night
        A drunken minstrel in his careless verse
Spoke the vile words that should not see the light,

---

1. sistrum: 摇鼓，由金属框架和可动横杆构成的古埃及打击
乐器。

他们将其伐倒，那里漆黑的小径
　　　藏有夜晚森林中的永生之物，
他们用高塔和大理石堆登上天空
　　　将他们寻欢作乐的城市建筑。

以洁白与非凡映衬四周的地表
　　　奢侈的穹顶和塔楼纷纷林立；
水晶和象牙，雍容华贵地笼罩
　　　穿透了不融之雪的尖锐锥体。

在那些长笛与摇鼓交响的厅堂，
　　　红酒和暴乱带来血色的污点；
不再有声音将古老的奇迹传唱，
　　　也没有眼睛回忆起山丘平原。

光阴荏苒，直到一个紫夜之时
　　　某位粗心的游方艺人因醉酒
说出了本不能见光的邪恶言词，

And stirr'd the shadows of an ancient curse.

Forests may fall, but not the dusk they shield;
So on the spot where that proud city stood,
The shuddering dawn no single stone reveal'd,
But fled the blackness of a primal wood.

246
树林

唤醒了阴霾之下远古的诅咒。

森林易倒，但其中的幽暗永存；
　　在那座傲慢之城立足的方位，
战栗的黎明来时没有一物留痕，
　　只飞过旧日树林留下的漆黑。

边区
The Outpost

发表于《培根随笔》1930 年春季刊。本诗的灵感来源是洛夫克拉夫特的伙伴爱德华·劳埃德·塞克里斯特所讲的故事，后者曾经亲身在津巴布韦的废墟中探索。

When evening cools the yellow stream,
    And shadows stalk the jungle's ways,
    Zimbabwe's palace flares ablaze
For a great King who fears to dream.

For he alone of all mankind
    Waded the swamp that serpents shun;
    And struggling toward the setting sun,
Came on the veldt that lies behind.

No other eyes had vented there
    Since eyes were lent for human sight—
    But there, as sunset turned to night,
He found the Elder Secret's lair.

Strange turrets rose beyond the plain,
    And walls and bastions spread around
    The distant domes that fouled the ground
Like leprous fungi after rain.

当黄色小溪随傍晚变得凉爽，

　　暗影在丛林之路上蹑足而行，

　　津巴布韦的宫殿里灯火通明

皆因那畏惧梦境的伟大君王。

因为人类中仅有他独自一员

　　曾前往巨蟒却步的沼泽跋涉；

　　并朝着西沉的落日长途奔波，

来到了地平线后的广袤草原。

没有另一双眼在那得到宣泄

　　因为眼眸适用于人间的景物——

　　但那里，当黄昏化入了夜幕，

他发现藏有远古秘密的巢穴。

平原的上方升起陌生的塔林，

　　而高墙和堡垒在其四周蔓延

　　远方的穹顶将整片地表污染

如同沐雨之后麻风病的真菌。

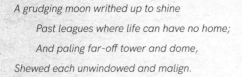

A grudging moon writhed up to shine
  Past leagues where life can have no home;
  And paling far-off tower and dome,
Shewed each unwindowed and malign.

Then he who in his boyhood ran
  Through vine-hung ruins free of fear,
  Trembled at what he saw—for here
Was no dead, ruined seat of man.

Inhuman shapes, half-seen, half-guessed,
  Half solid and half ether-spawned,
  Seethed down from starless voids that yawned
In heav'n, to these blank walls of pest.

And voidward from that pest-mad zone
  Amorphous hordes seethed darkly back,
  Their dim claws laden with the wrack
Of things that men have dreamed and known.

扭动的月光毫不情愿地照映

　　洒满了生命无法居住的地带；

　　遥远的高塔与穹顶一片惨白，

每一幢都无窗并险恶地现形。

他虽然曾在孩提时代奔跑着

　　无畏地穿越挂满青藤的废墟，

　　却因所见之物颤抖——因为此地

不同于人类荒弃的死亡之座。

非人的影迹，一半明一半暗，

　　一半是实体一半由以太组构，

　　涌出自无星的虚空中的裂口

从高天落向可憎的空白墙垣。

而从疯狂可憎之地向着虚空

　　奇形怪状的群体阴沉地回归，

　　它们暗色的利爪紧握的湮废

来自人类在梦中熟知的种种。

The ancient Fishers from Outside [1] —
 Were there not tales the high-priest told,
 Of how they found the worlds of old,
And took what pelf their fancy spied?

Their hidden, dread-ringed outposts brood
 Upon a million worlds of space;
 Abhorred by every living race,
Yet scatheless in their solitude.

Sweating with fright, the watcher crept
 Back to the swamp that serpents shun,
 So that he lay, by rise of sun,
Safe in the palace where he slept.

None saw him leave, or come at dawn,
 Nor does his flesh bear any mark
 Of what he met in that curst dark—
Yet from his sleep all peace has gone.

---

1. Fishers from Outside: 洛夫克拉夫特在与海泽尔·希尔德合著的小说《有翼死神》中再次提到了这个短语，"他们说那些巨石比人类还要古老，曾经作为边区或巢穴归属于'星海钓客'——天知道那是什么——以及邪神撒托古亚与克苏鲁。"

那群从远古而来的星海钓客——

　　　高阶祭司的故事并不曾提到，

　　　它们是如何将上古之世寻找，

又取走了哪些被觊觎的财帛？

它们恐怖环绕下的隐秘边区

　　　散布于宇宙间上百万个世界；

　　　被每个有灵的种群深恶痛绝，

却在它们的独居中平安无虞。

惊恐而流汗，国王手脚并用

　　　回到了那片巨蟒却步的沼泽，

　　　他躺在那里，太阳升起之刻，

平安地置身于他入梦的王宫。

无人见他离去或在黎明归来，

　　　他的肉体上也没有丝毫痕迹

　　　代表了诅咒的黑暗里的遭遇——

但他睡梦中的安宁不复存在。

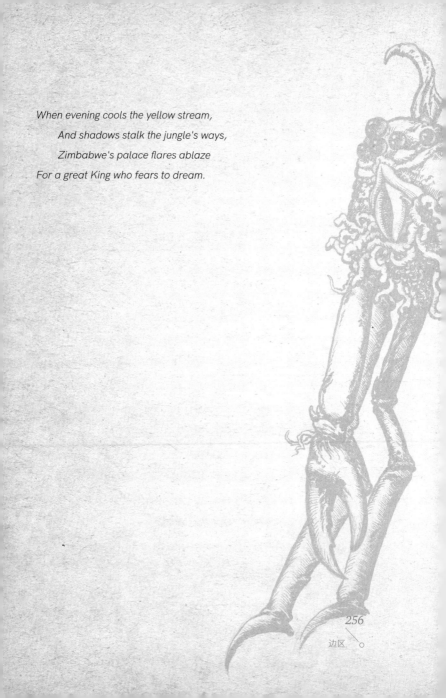

When evening cools the yellow stream,
    And shadows stalk the jungle's ways,
    Zimbabwe's palace flares ablaze
For a great King who fears to dream.

当黄色小溪随傍晚变得凉爽，

　　暗影在丛林之路上蹑足而行，

　　津巴布韦的宫殿里灯火通明

皆因那畏惧梦境的伟大君王。

古道
The Ancient Track

发表于《诡丽奇谭》1930 年三月刊。

There was no hand to hold me back
That night I found the ancient track
Over the hill, and strained to see
The fields that teased my memory.
This tree, that wall—I knew them well,
And all the roofs and orchards fell
Familiarly upon my mind
As from a past not far behind.
I knew what shadows would be cast
When the late moon came up at last
From back of Zaman's Hill[1] , and how
The vale would shine three hours from now.
And when the path grew steep and high,
And seemed to end against the sky,
I had no fear of what might rest

---

1. Zaman's Hill: 扎曼之丘，择人而噬的巨大活体山峰。

再也没有手掌能够将我阻挠

自从那个夜晚我发现了古道

在山丘之上，并且费力地看见

嘲弄着我的记忆的那片地面。

这棵树，那堵墙——我熟悉它们，

而所有屋顶和果园纷纷降临

无比亲昵地坠落在我的心头

它们所属的过去仍相隔不久。

我知道将会投下怎样的荫翳

当迟来的月亮最后终于升起

在扎曼之丘的背后，又是怎样

山谷将会闪耀三小时之长。

当那条道路变得陡峭又高耸，

似乎到最后已经触及了天空，

我毫不畏惧有什么正在沉睡

Beyond that silhouetted crest.
Straight on I walked, while all the night
Grew pale with phosphorescent light,
And wall and farmhouse gable glowed
Unearthly by the climbing road.
There was the milestone that I knew—
Two miles to Dunwich [1]—now the view
Of distant spire and roofs would dawn
With ten more upward paces gone...

There was no hand to hold me back
That night I found the ancient track,
And reached the crest to see outspread
A valley of the lost and dead:
And over Zaman's Hill the horn
Of a malignant moon was born,
To light the weeds and vines that grew
On ruined walls I never knew.
The fox-fire glowed in field and bog,
And unknown waters spewed a fog
Whose curling talons mocked the thought

---

1. Dunwich: 敦威治，克苏鲁神话中的虚构地点，与世隔绝的
美国马萨诸塞州林中小镇，充满谋杀、乱伦与邪神崇拜传统。

于现出轮廓的山顶上方之位。

我向前直行，直到整片夜色

被荧光闪闪的灯火变得微弱，

而墙壁和农庄山墙放出光彩

在上坡路一旁如同来自地外。

我知道这里曾有一块里程石——

"距敦威治两英里"——眼中此时

远处的尖塔和屋顶即将拂曙

只需要向上方继续踏出十步……

再也没有手掌能够将我阻挠

自从那个夜晚我发现了古道，

并且抵达了山顶以尽收眼底

失落并死气沉沉的山谷地区：

在扎曼之丘上方那号角一般

满怀着恶意的新月已然降诞，

照亮的野草与藤条潜滋暗长

于我一无所知的那残壁断墙。

狐火在田野和沼泽之间闪烁，

而不知名的水域将雾气喷薄

它那缭绕的利爪嘲弄着脑中

That I had ever known this spot.
Too well I saw from the mad scene
That my loved past had never been—
Nor was I now upon the trail
Descending to that long-dead vale.
Around was fog—ahead, the spray
Of star-streams in the Milky Way...
There was no hand to hold me back
That night I found the ancient track.

264

古道

我对于这个地点怀有的旧情。

我清楚地看到那疯狂的景致

而我所眷恋的过去从未如此——

也不存在我此刻立足的道路

向下延伸至死去已久的山谷。

四周雾气笼罩——前方的水花

自银河之中群星的溪流落下……

再也没有手掌能够将我阻挠

自从那个夜晚我发现了古道。

信使
The Messenger

致贝特朗·K.哈特先生
To Bertrand K. Hart, Esq.

发表于《诡丽奇谭》1938年七月刊。贝特朗·K.哈特是《普罗维登斯日报》的编辑，曾将本诗完整地刊登在他的专栏中。哈特在阅读小说《克苏鲁的呼唤》后，发现文中人物威尔科克斯的住处罗得岛州普罗维登斯托马斯街7号，正是他在现实生活中曾经住过的地方。哈特因而打趣："……我将不得安宁，直到加入幽魂和食尸鬼的行列，我已经通过在它巴恩斯街的门口采取直接报复的手段放倒了至少一只巨大而永生的鬼灵……我想我应该教会它如何在每当凌晨三点的时钟尖锐响起时以不和谐的小调呻吟，伴着钟声阵阵。"

The thing, he said, would come that night at three

From the old churchyard on the hill below;

But crouching by an oak fires wholesome glow,

I tried to tell myself it could not be.

Surely, I mused, it was a pleasantry

Devised by one who did not truly know

The Elder Sign [1] , bequeathed from long ago,

That sets the fumbling forms of darkness free.

He had not meant it—no—but still I lit

Another lamp as starry Leo climbed

Out of the Seekonk [2] , and a steeple chimed

Three—and the firelight faded, bit by bit.

Then at the door that cautious rattling came—

And the mad truth devoured me like a flame!

1. The Elder Sign: 旧神之印，克苏鲁神话中用于驱逐神话生物的符号，但往往收效甚微。

2. Seekonk: 锡康克，美国马萨诸塞州城市，与罗得岛州普罗维登斯接壤。

他说午夜三点会出现某种东西

自下方山顶的古老教堂墓园而至；

但在橡木炉火和暖的光芒中伏伺，

我试着告诉自己此话不足为据。

我思忖那一定只是在诙谐打趣

构想出此话之人根本一无所知

旧神之印，自远古流传后世，

能使黑暗的笨拙身影扬长而去。

他并未这样嘱托——但我依旧点燃

另一盏灯火，当狮子座的繁星上升

在锡康克城外，而钟楼终于奏鸣

三声——光亮也一点点归于黯淡。

门外怪异的窸窣响动逐渐逼近——

疯狂的真相如同烈焰般将我侵吞！

Fungi from Yuggoth

来自犹格斯的真菌

这组十四行诗创作于 1929 年 12 月 27 日至 1930 年 1 月 4 日，作者在生前从未计划将其结集出版，而是将每首独立发表或是赠予他人，直到 1943 年阿卡姆之屋出版的《翻越睡梦之墙》才完整收录了全篇。黑暗行星犹格斯的概念在组诗中被首次提出，而在组诗完成一个多月后，美国天文学家克莱德·汤博发现了冥王星的存在。洛夫克拉夫特以少有的兴奋在给詹姆斯·F. 莫顿的一封信中提及这次天文发现："你怎么看这颗新行星？太酷了！！！也许那就是犹格斯。"自此洛夫克拉夫特笔下的犹格斯开始演变为冥王星的代名词，"来自犹格斯的真菌"也被视为古老的高智慧外星种族米-戈的别称。

书卷
The Book

发表于《幻想迷》1934 年十月刊。作者曾经重写过组诗中的前三首十四行诗，使它们形成一个连贯的故事。而废弃的前三首诗的原文可能在改写后成为小说《书》。

The place was dark and dusty and half-lost
In tangles of old alleys near the quays,
Reeking of strange things brought in from the seas,
And with queer curls of fog that west winds tossed.
Small lozenge panes, obscured by smoke and frost,
Just shewed the books, in piles like twisted trees,
Rotting from floor to roof—congeries
Of crumbling elder lore at little cost.

I entered, charmed, and from a cobwebbed heap
Took up the nearest tome and thumbed it through,
Trembling at curious words that seemed to keep
Some secret, monstrous if one only knew.
Then, looking for some seller old in craft,
I could find nothing but a voice that laughed.

此处昏暗蒙尘，半已遗失于
码头边错综复杂的古老巷陌，
海洋中古怪生物的恶臭传播，
迷雾诡异的涡流随西风汇聚。
菱形的小窗，被烟尘与寒霜遮蔽，
勉强映出书卷，如扭曲的树木成摞，
从地面到屋顶都已腐朽——堆积着
古老而衰朽的知识，而价格颇低。

我进门，入神，从布满蛛网的书堆上
拿起最近的一本典籍并快速翻阅，
惊颤于这些怪异的字词似乎在掩藏
某种秘密，有着不为人知的罪孽。
随后，我将某位经验老到的卖家寻找，
却一无所获，只听见一个声音的嘲笑。

追逐
Pursuit

发表于《幻想迷》1934 年十月刊。

I held the book beneath my coat, at pains
To hide the thing from sight in such a place;
Hurrying through the ancient harbor lanes
With often-turning head and nervous pace.
Dull, furtive windows in old tottering brick
Peered at me oddly as I hastened by,
And thinking what they sheltered, I grew sick
For a redeeming glimpse of clean blue sky.

No one had seen me take the thing — but still
A blank laugh echoed in my whirling head,
And I could guess what nighted worlds of ill
Lurked in that volume I had coveted.
The way grew strange—the walls alike and madding—
And far behind me, unseen feet were padding.

我将书卷藏在外套之下，竭力想要
让此物在这种地方不引起注目；
行色匆匆穿过这古老海港的街道
不停扭头回望，加紧了脚步。
衰老的危墙上阴森诡谲的窗口
古怪地凝视着我快步经过，
想到它们背后的秘密，我不禁渴求
举目纯净的蓝天并获得解脱。

无人看到我带走此物——但是时时
空洞的笑声在我眩晕的脑中响起，
我能够想象是多么丑恶的黑暗之世
在我贪求的这部书卷之中藏匿。
道路变得陌生——墙壁相似又疯狂——
而远远在我身后，无形的脚步发出轻响。

钥匙
The Key

发表于《幻想迷》1935 年一月刊。

I do not know what windings in the waste
Of those strange sea-lanes brought me home once more,
But on my porch I trembled, white with haste
To get inside and bolt the heavy door.
I had the book that told the hidden way
Across the void and through the space-hung screens
That hold the undimensioned worlds at bay,
And keep lost aeons to their own demesnes.

At last the key was mine to those vague visions
Of sunset spires and twilight woods that brood
Dim in the gulfs beyond this earth's precisions,
Lurking as memories of infinitude.
The key was mine, but as I sat there mumbling,
The attic window shook with a faint fumbling.

我不知道荒郊中的哪一条曲径
从陌生的海滨小巷带我再度归返，
在走廊上我面色惨白，颤抖着匆匆
进入室内，并将沉重的大门紧掩。
手中的书卷指明有暗藏的天阶
跨越虚空并穿过宇宙间的巨幕，
它牢牢牵制住未曾标注的世界，
并限定失落的万古于各自所属。

最终我得到了钥匙，通往幻境里
日落的塔尖和暮光中冥思的树林
它们在地球不能测度的深渊消匿，
作为对于无限的记忆而暗自藏身。
我得到了钥匙，而当我坐在这喃喃不休，
阁楼的窗户受到轻微的触摸并颤抖。

识别
Recognitions

发表于《飘风》1936 年十二月刊。

The day had come again, when as a child
I saw—just once—that hollow of old oaks,
Grey with a ground-mist that enfolds and chokes
The slinking shapes which madness has defiled.
It was the same—an herbage rank and wild
Clings round an altar whose carved sign invokes
That Nameless One to whom a thousand smokes
Rose, aeons gone, from unclean towers up-piled.

I saw the body spread on that dank stone,
And knew those things which feasted were not men;
I knew this strange, grey world was not my own,
But Yuggoth, past the starry voids—and then
The body shrieked at me with a dead cry,
And all too late I knew that it was I!

这一日再度来临，当我仍是孩童，

我曾——仅一次——在老橡树林的空地见过，

灰暗中地面的雾气笼罩并窒息了

那些被疯狂所玷污的鬼祟身影。

一切恰似当初——杂乱生长的草丛

托起一个祭坛，其上的雕文召唤着

某位无名之神，千缕的浓烟为此者

升起，万古逝去，在不洁的群塔上空。

我看到一具躯体在阴冷的石上瘫软，

并认出那些享受饕餮之徒并非常人；

我知道这陌生灰暗的世界并非我的故园，

而是犹格斯，远隔深空的繁星——转瞬

那具躯体对我尖声发出垂死的哭泣，

一切已经太迟，我认出那是自己！

归乡
Homecoming

发表于《幻想迷》1935 年一月刊。

The daemon said that he would take me home
To the pale, shadowy land I half recalled
As a high place of stair and terrace, walled
With marble balustrades that sky-winds comb,
While miles below a maze of dome on dome
And tower on tower beside a sea lies sprawled.
Once more, he told me, I would stand enthralled
On those old heights, and hear the far-off foam.

All this he promised, and through sunset's gate
He swept me, past the lapping lakes of flame,
And red-gold thrones of gods without a name
Who shriek in fear at some impending fate.
Then a black gulf with sea-sounds in the night:
"Here was your home," he mocked, "when you had sight!"

那个恶魔说他会带我回到家中

回到我半已遗忘的苍白阴暗之地

在阶梯与露台林立的高处，外壁

大理石的围栏栉沐着天际的风，

而数英里下的迷宫内一层层穹顶

和一重重塔楼毗邻着蔓延的海域。

他再一次告诉我，我会着迷地伫立

在那些古老的高台，倾听遥远的泡影。

他承诺这一切，并由落日的大门

推我入内，穿过烈焰拍岸的湖泊，

以及无名的诸神们金红色的宝座

祂们悚然惊呼于某种迫近的命运。

最后是一片夜潮回荡的漆黑峡湾：

　　"这就是你的家，"他嘲笑，"如果你能看见！"

神灯
The Lamp

发表于《飘风》1931 年三月刊。

We found the lamp inside those hollow cliffs

Whose chiseled sign no priest in Thebes [1] could read,

And from whose caverns frightened hieroglyphs

Warned every living creature of earth's breed.

No more was there—just that one brazen bowl

With traces of a curious oil within;

Fretted with some obscurely patterned scroll,

And symbols hinting vaguely of strange sin.

Little the fears of forty centuries meant

To us as we bore off our slender spoil,

And when we scanned it in our darkened tent

We struck a match to test the ancient oil.

It blazed—great God!... But the vast shapes we saw

In that mad flash have seared our lives with awe.

---

1. Thebes: 忒拜，又译底比斯，拥有众多神庙、宫殿和陵墓
的古埃及都城，被荷马称为"百门之都"。

我们发现神灯之地是那凹陷的峭壁

其上的刻印忒拜祭司中无人能懂，

在它岩洞中的象形文字满怀着恐惧

警示着每一个地球孕育出的生灵。

此地别无他物——仅有一个青铜灯盏

里面似乎盛着离奇古怪的油膏；

镌刻有某种纹路令人费解的图案，

以及隐隐暗示着诡秘罪恶的符号。

历经了四十个世纪的悚惧也无法

阻止我们把这个微薄的收获带走，

当我们在昏暗的帐篷中将其检查

我们擦亮火柴以试验古老的灯油。

它亮了——神啊！……但我们眼前的巨大形象

在疯狂的闪光中以巨力使我们的生命凋亡。

扎曼之丘
Zaman's Hill

发表于《飘风》1934 年十月刊。

The great hill hung close over the old town,
A precipice against the main street's end;
Green, tall, and wooded, looking darkly down
Upon the steeple at the highway bend.
Two hundred years the whispers had been heard
About what happened on the man-shunned slope—
Tales of an oddly mangled deer or bird,
Or of lost boys whose kin had ceased to hope.

One day the mail-man found no village there,
Nor were its folk or houses seen again;
People came out from Aylesbury [1] to stare—
Yet they all told the mail-man it was plain
That he was mad for saying he had spied
The great hill's gluttonous eyes, and jaws stretched wide.

---

1. Aylesbury: 艾尔斯伯里，位于美国马萨诸塞州中北部的虚
构小镇，离敦威治不远。

那座庞大的山丘在古镇的上方低悬，
紧靠主大街的尽头形成一处陡崖；
苍郁，高耸，树木繁茂，阴沉地俯瞰
下方交通干线转弯之处的尖塔。
两百年之中不断地有流言传述
那令人却步的山坡上发生的事情——
关于某只被离奇撕碎的飞鸟或鹿，
或家人们放弃了希望的失踪孩童。

某日邮递员发现村镇已不复存在，
也无法再次见到它的居民或屋舍；
人们从艾尔斯伯里为一睹而来——
但他们告诉邮递员事情再清楚不过
他一定是疯了才会声称自己曾经窥透
那座庞大山丘贪婪的眼球，和张开的血盆大口。

港口
The Port

发表于《飘风》1930 年十一月刊。

Ten miles from Arkham [1] I had struck the trail

That rides the cliff-edge over Boynton Beach [2] ,

And hoped that just at sunset I could reach

The crest that looks on Innsmouth [3] in the vale.

Far out at sea was a retreating sail,

White as hard years of ancient winds could bleach,

But evil with some portent beyond speech,

So that I did not wave my hand or hail.

Sails out of Innsmouth! Echoing old renown

Of long-dead times. But now a too-swift night

Is closing in, and I have reached the height

Whence I so often scan the distant town.

The spires and roofs are there—but look! The gloom

Sinks on dark lanes, as lightless as the tomb!

---

1. Arkham: 阿卡姆，克苏鲁神话中的虚构地点，一座位于美
国马萨诸塞州的黑暗城镇。阿卡姆是密斯卡托尼克大学、魔女
之家、刽子手山丘等著名场所的所在地，神话生物频频在此处
出没。

2. Boynton Beach: 博因顿海滩，与美国佛罗里达州城市同名
的虚构地点。

3. Innsmouth: 印斯茅斯，克苏鲁神话中虚构的美国马萨诸塞
州港口城镇，在 1812 年美英战争后衰落，成为扭曲的深潜者
盘踞之地。

在阿卡姆十英里外我改变路线

以穿过博因顿海滩上方的峭壁，

希望自己能够在日落时分赶抵

俯瞰着谷地中印斯茅斯的山巅。

远方的海面有一抹远去的船帆，

被荒年的远古之风漂染得洁白无比，

但它蕴藏的邪恶预兆超越了言语，

所以我并没有挥动手臂或呼喊。

印斯茅斯的离帆！这古老荣光的回响

来自长逝的年代。但是黑夜太过迅速

地笼罩而来，而我抵达了那个高处

像往常一样在此把遥远的城镇眺望。

尖塔和屋顶依然如旧——但是看清！阴影

沉入了黑暗的街巷，就像黯淡无光的坟茔！

庭院
The Courtyard

发表于《诡丽奇谭》1930 年九月刊。本诗的情节是对小说《他》的高度总结。

It was the city I had known before;

The ancient, leprous town where mongrel throngs

Chant to strange gods, and beat unhallowed gongs

In crypts beneath foul alleys near the shore.

The rotting, fish-eyed houses leered at me

From where they leaned, drunk and half-animate,

As edging through the filth I passed the gate

To the black courtyard [1] where the man would be.

The dark walls closed me in, and loud I cursed

That ever I had come to such a den,

When suddenly a score of windows burst

Into wild light, and swarmed with dancing men:

Mad, soundless revels of the dragging dead—

And not a corpse had either hands or head!

---

1. the black courtyard: 这座庭院坐落于纽约曼哈顿佩里街 93 号。

这座城市我在从前便已知晓；
古老的麻风集镇中有无数杂种
称颂怪异的神祇，亵渎的锣声
充满海岸旁恶臭小巷下的地窖。
用冷眼将我睨视的腐朽房垣
在原地斜倚，酩酊又死气沉沉，
而我穿越过污秽进入了大门
来到与人约定过的漆黑庭院。

黝黯的墙将我包围，我大声咒骂
自己竟会来到这样一个黑窝，
突然间二十扇窗户一同爆发
出狂乱的光，并且挤满了舞者：
行尸走肉们寂静而疯狂的庆祝——
而没有一具尸体有着双手或头颅！

驯鸽人
The Pigeon-Flyers

在结集出版前未独立发表。作者本人评价："对于此诗的理解需要通过其与纽约'地狱厨房'贫民窟真实风俗的相似性入手，在那里堆筑篝火和驯鸽是年轻人的两种主要的娱乐活动。"

They took me slumming, where gaunt walls of brick

Bulge outward with a viscous stored-up evil,

And twisted faces, thronging foul and thick,

Wink messages to alien god and devil.

A million fires were blazing in the streets,

And from flat roofs a furtive few would fly

Bedraggled birds into the yawning sky

While hidden drums droned on with measured beats.

I knew those fires were brewing monstrous things,

And that those birds of space had been Outside—

I guessed to what dark planet's crypts they plied,

And what they brought from Thog [1] beneath their wings.

The others laughed—till struck too mute to speak

By what they glimpsed in one bird's evil beak.

---

1. Thog: 索格，黑暗行星犹格斯的双子卫星之一。

他们带我到贫民窟，那里破败的砖墙
积攒了浓稠的邪恶而向外凸起，
而污秽并拥挤成群的扭曲面庞
向异域的神和魔鬼暗送着讯息。
千万道火光闪耀在巷尾街头，
平坦的屋顶有可疑的人群放飞
升入广阔天空的肮脏的鸟类，
而无形之鼓嗡鸣着低缓的节奏。

我知道这些火光酝酿着某种丑恶，
以及这些空间中的飞鸟曾前往异界——
我猜想它们涌向哪颗黑暗行星的地穴，
还有它们翅膀下从索格带回了什么。
旁人付之哄笑——直到震惊得无法说出
他们在一只邪恶的鸟喙中所见之物。

井
The Well

发表于 1930 年 5 月 14 日的《普罗维登斯日报》。

Farmer Seth Atwood [1] was past eighty when

He tried to sink that deep well by his door,

With only Eb to help him bore and bore.

We laughed, and hoped he'd soon be sane again.

And yet, instead, young Eb went crazy, too,

So that they shipped him to the county farm.

Seth bricked the well-mouth up as tight as glue—

Then hacked an artery in his gnarled left arm.

After the funeral we felt bound to get

Out to that well and rip the bricks away,

But all we saw were iron hand-holds set

Down a black hole deeper than we could say.

And yet we put the bricks back—for we found

The hole too deep for any line to sound.

---

1. Atwood: 阿特伍德，这个姓氏也出现在小说《疯狂山脉》
与《墓园里的恐怖》之中。

农夫塞斯·阿特伍德那时年过八十
却想要挖掘自家门前的那口深井，
只有埃布帮着他无休无止地凿洞，
我们嘲笑着，希望他尽快恢复理智。
但恰恰相反，年轻的埃布也陷入疯狂，
于是被人们运送前往郡属的农田。
塞斯用砖将井口密封得像胶水一样——
然后切断了粗糙左臂上的一截血管。

葬礼过后我们觉得有必要前去
那座井的旁边并移除那些砖头，
但我们只看见一排铁质的爬梯
消失在说不清多深的漆黑洞口。
于是我们将砖头复位——因为我们发觉
这个洞的深度无法被任何绳子鉴别。

咆哮者
The Howler

发表于《飘风》1932 年十一月刊。

They told me not to take the Briggs' Hill path
That used to be the highroad through to Zoar[1]
For Goody Watkins, hanged in seventeen-four,
Had left a certain monstrous aftermath.
Yet when I disobeyed, and had in view
The vine-hung cottage by the great rock slope,
I could not think of elms or hempen rope,
But wondered why the house still seemed so new.

Stopping a while to watch the fading day,
I heard faint howls, as from a room upstairs,
When through the ivied panes one sunset ray
Struck in, and caught the howler unawares.
I glimpsed—and ran in frenzy from the place,
And from a four-pawed thing with human face.

---

1. Zoar: 琐珥，美国马萨诸塞州西北部城镇。

他们告诉我别走布里格斯的山路

那里曾是前往琐珥的主要通道，

因为古迪·沃特金斯于一七○四年受绞，

在此留下了某种骇人听闻的遗毒。

但是我没有听从，然后眼前面临

巨大岩山下挂满了藤蔓的屋舍，

我没有在意榆树或大麻的绳索，

却好奇这间房子为何如此崭新。

驻足片刻以观望消退的白昼之时，

我听到隐约的咆哮，来自楼上某一间房，

这时一束余晖穿过青藤覆盖的窗子

映入屋内，将咆哮者猝不及防地照亮。

我瞄了一眼——然后发疯似的逃离了此地，

以及那个四脚爬行却长着人脸的东西。

西方之国
Hesperia

发表于《诡丽奇谭》1930 年十月刊。

The winter sunset, flaming beyond spires
And chimneys half-detached from this dull sphere,
Opens great gates to some forgotten year
Of elder splendours and divine desires.
Expectant wonders burn in those rich fires,
Adventure-fraught, and not untinged with fear;
A row of sphinxes where the way leads clear
Toward walls and turrets quivering to far lyres.

It is the land where beauty's meaning flowers;
Where every unplaced memory has a source;
Where the great river Time begins its course
Down the vast void in starlit streams of hours.
Dreams bring us close—but ancient lore repeats
That human tread has never soiled these streets.

冬日的夕照，熊熊高踞在塔尖

和若即若离于昏暗天穹的烟囱之上，

洞开了雄伟大门后被遗忘的时光

当中古老的盛景和神圣的欲念。

未来的奇迹绽放于这些烈焰，

满载着冒险，并未沾染任何恐慌；

一列狮身人面像的道路分明通往

被远方里拉琴撼动的塔楼与墙垣。

在这片土地，美即是寓意深刻的花朵；

在这里每一段无定的记忆都有源头；

在这里岁月的长河开始了它的奔流

化作星光下时辰的小溪穿越虚空寥廓。

梦境带我们接近——但远古的传说复述

人类的足迹从未将这些街道玷污。

星风
Star-Winds

发表于《诡丽奇谭》1930 年九月刊。

It is a certain hour of twilight glooms,

Mostly in autumn, when the star-wind pours

Down hilltop streets, deserted out-of-doors,

But shewing early lamplight from snug rooms.

The dead leaves rush in strange, fantastic twists,

And chimney-smoke whirls round with alien grace,

Heeding geometries of outer space,

While Fomalhaut [1] *peers in through southward mists.*

This is the hour when moonstruck poets know

What fungi sprout in Yuggoth, and what scents

And tints of flowers fill Nithon's [2] *continents,*

Such as in no poor earthly garden blow.

Yet for each dream these winds to us convey,

A dozen more of ours they sweep away!

---

1. Fomalhaut: 北落师门，距离地球约 25.1 光年的白色主序恒星，在克苏鲁神话中是旧日支配者克图格亚的居住地。

2. Nithon: 尼松，黑暗行星犹格斯的卫星，云雾缭绕并长满真菌。

在昏暗暮光下的某个特定时刻，
大多是秋季，当星风倾盆如雨
下落在山顶的街道，那露天荒地
却映出温暖房间中初上的灯火。
纷纷落叶异常怪诞地飞速打转，
炊烟带着诡秘的优雅来回转身，
它们被外层空间的几何图案吸引，
当北落师门透过南行的雾向下窥看。

此时此刻痴心妄想的诗人明白
哪些犹格斯的真菌，以及哪些幽香
和花朵的异彩弥漫在尼松的陆上，
它们不在尘世间低贱的花园盛开。
只是星风为我们带来的每一个梦，
都将我们十二倍的旧梦一扫而空！

极南之地
Antarktos

发表于《诡丽奇谭》1930 年十一月刊。诗歌的题目是洛夫克拉夫特为指代南极地区而造的希腊语词汇。

Deep in my dream the great bird whispered queerly
Of the black cone amid the polar waste;
Pushing above the ice-sheet lone and drearly,
By storm-crazed aeons battered and defaced.
Hither no living earth-shapes take their courses,
And only pale auroras and faint suns
Glow on that pitted rock, whose primal sources
Are guessed at dimly by the Elder Ones.

If men should glimpse it, they would merely wonder
What tricky mound of Nature's build they spied;
But the bird told of vaster parts, that under
The mile-deep ice-shroud crouch and brood and bide.
God help the dreamer whose mad visions shew
Those dead eyes set in crystal gulfs below!

巨鸟在我的梦境深处奇异地低诉

四面包围着极地荒原的黑色圆锥；

在阴郁孤独的冰盖上突刺而出，

被万古的狂风暴雪重创并损毁。

这里没有活的地球物种顺应自然，

只有苍白的极光和微弱的日轮

映照在坑洼的石锥之上，它的起源

被模糊地猜测是那些古老者们。

如果人类瞥见，他们仅仅会诧异

自己发现了自然何样的鬼斧神工；

但是巨鸟透露更大的秘密深藏于

数英里的冰层下潜伏、孵化并久等。

神灵保佑，若入梦者疯狂的视线揭露

那些晶莹裂谷下存在的死亡之眸！

窗
The Window

发表于《飘风》1931 年 4 月的特刊。

The house was old, with tangled wings outthrown,

Of which no one could ever half keep track,

And in a small room somewhat near the back

Was an odd window sealed with ancient stone.

There, in a dream-plagued childhood, quite alone

I used to go, where night reigned vague and black;

Parting the cobwebs with a curious lack

Of fear, and with a wonder each time grown.

One later day I brought the masons there

To find what view my dim forbears had shunned,

But as they pierced the stone, a rush of air

Burst from the alien voids that yawned beyond.

They fled—but I peered through and found unrolled

All the wild worlds of which my dreams had told.

这栋古老房屋的扭曲侧翼向外延伸，

无人能将其中发生的事情加以记录，

在某个背阴一面狭小的房间内部

有一扇奇怪的窗被远古的石块封存。

那里，我在梦境缠身的童年，曾孤身

多次前往，夜晚所辖模糊与黑暗之处；

将蜘蛛网分开，出乎意料地并不

感到恐惧，只有逐次递增的疑问。

之后的某日我带了几位石匠同往

以探寻我不明的先祖想逃避何种异景，

但是当他们凿开那块石头，一股气浪

从头顶张口的陌生虚空中向外喷涌。

他们逃走了——但我向内凝望并且发觉

梦境中曾经揭示的每一个狂野世界。

回忆
A Memory

在结集出版前未独立发表。

There were great steppes, and rocky table-lands
Stretching half-limitless in starlit night,
With alien campfires shedding feeble light
On beasts with tinkling bells, in shaggy bands.
Far to the south the plain sloped low and wide
To a dark zigzag line of wall that lay
Like a huge python of some primal day
Which endless time had chilled and petrified.

I shivered oddly in the cold, thin air,
And wondered where I was and how I came,
When a cloaked form against a campfire's glare
Rose and approached, and called me by my name.
Staring at that dead face beneath the hood,
I ceased to hope—because I understood.

那里有广阔的草原，布满岩石的台地
几乎漫无边际地伸入星光下的夜色，
异乡的营火将微弱的光芒洒落
在铃声叮当的兽群上，那蓬乱的集体。
平原在遥远的南方整体向下倾斜
直至一堵蜿蜒伸展的黑色高墙
如同某条来自古老年代的巨蟒
被冰封并石化于那无尽的岁月。

我在寒冷稀薄的空气中诡然抖动
疑惑自己身在何处又何以至此，
这时背对着营火的斗篷下的人影
起身并接近，并呼唤出我的名字。
直视那兜帽下掩藏的死者面目，
我放弃了希望——因为我顿然醒悟。

阴花园
The Gardens of Yin

发表于《飘风》1932 年三月刊。本诗的灵感来源是罗伯特 · W. 钱伯斯在《月亮的制造者》中塑造的虚构中国城市易安。在 1930 年夏，洛夫克拉夫特盛赞弗吉尼亚州里士满市的梅蒙德公园为现实生活中的阴花园。

Beyond that wall, whose ancient masonry
Reached almost to the sky in moss-thick towers,
There would be terraced gardens, rich with flowers,
And flutter of bird and butterfly and bee.
There would be walks, and bridges arching over
Warm lotos-pools reflecting temple eaves,
And cherry-trees with delicate boughs and leaves
Against a pink sky where the herons hover.

All would be there, for had not old dreams flung
Open the gate to that stone-lanterned maze
Where drowsy streams spin out their winding ways,
Trailed by green vines from bending branches hung?
I hurried—but when the wall rose, grim and great,
I found there was no longer any gate.

越过那道墙，它古老的砖石构筑

几乎触及长满青苔的高塔上的天空，

那里有着阶梯式的花园，繁花茂盛，

以及鸟儿、蝴蝶和蜜蜂在翩翩飞舞。

那里有着小径，和桥梁弓身横穿

倒映着寺庙屋檐的温暖的莲池，

以及樱花树上纤柔的枝条与叶子

映衬着白鹭盘旋的粉红色长天。

一切都在那里，因为若是旧梦没有

猛然打开通往那石灯笼迷宫的大门

沉寂诸河蜿蜒的走势该向何处延伸，

当弯弯枝头上垂下的青藤紧随其后？

我加快步伐——但是当墙升起，冰冷又宽广，

我发现所有的大门都已经不知去向。

钟
The Bells

发表于《诡丽奇谭》1930 年十二月刊。

Year after year I heard that faint, far ringing
Of deep-toned bells on the black midnight wind;
Peals from no steeple I could ever find,
But strange, as if across some great void winging.
I searched my dreams and memories for a clue,
And thought of all the chimes my visions carried;
Of quiet Innsmouth, where the white gulls tarried
Around an ancient spire that once I knew.

Always perplexed I heard those far notes falling,
Till one March night the bleak rain splashing cold
Beckoned me back through gateways of recalling
To elder towers where the mad clappers tolled.
They tolled—but from the sunless tides that pour
Through sunken valleys on the sea's dead floor.

年复一年我听到微弱的遥远声响

由浑厚沉钟飘入漆黑的午夜之风；

没有任何尖塔能够传来这种长鸣，

如此诡秘，似在跨越虚空地飞翔。

我找遍了梦境和回忆将线索寻求，

并回想我幻觉中存在的所有磬音；

和沉寂的印斯茅斯，那里白鸥降临

在一座我曾熟知的古老高塔四周。

我总是茫然聆听那些坠落的音符，

直到三月的某晚阴雨冰冷地飘洒

呼唤我重新穿过了追忆的门户

来到疯狂的钟摆敲响中的群塔。

它们敲响——但源头那无光的潮水漫溢

深海死亡岩床上凹陷的谷底。

夜魇
Night-Gaunts

　　发表于 1930 年 3 月 26 日的《普罗维登斯日报》。夜魇是洛夫克拉夫特自五岁经历了外婆的死亡后便开始在梦中见到的诡异物种，也是克苏鲁神话中的重要种族。

Out of what crypt they crawl, I cannot tell,

But every night I see the rubbery things,

Black, horned, and slender, with membraneous wings,

And tails that bear the bifid barb of hell.

They come in legions on the north wind's swell,

With obscene clutch that titillates and stings,

Snatching me off on monstrous voyagings

To grey worlds hidden deep in nightmare's well.

Over the jagged peaks of Thok they sweep,

Heedless of all the cries I try to make,

And down the nether pits to that foul lake

Where the puffed shoggoths [1] splash in doubtful sleep.

But oh! If only they would make some sound,

Or wear a face where faces should be found!

---

1. shoggoth: 修格斯，克苏鲁神话中的虚构种族，形态不定的黏液状生物，具有模拟其他生物的能力。

它们从哪座地穴爬出，我一无所知，
但每夜我都看到这些橡胶状的形体，
漆黑，长角，瘦削，生有膜质的飞翼
和如同地狱的双头叉一样的尾刺。
它们随着北风的涌动成群而至，
用可憎的爪子带给人瘙痒刺激，
劫持我踏上那骇人听闻的羁旅
前往噩梦的井下深藏的灰暗之世。

它们在索克崎岖不平的山峰上翻飞，
毫不在意我试图发出的声声尖叫，
并穿过下界的深渊来到恶臭的湖沼
肿胀的修格斯在可疑的休眠中入水。
但是啊！希望它们能够发出一些声响，
或在本该是面部的位置长有一张脸庞！

奈亚拉托提普

Ayarſathotep

　　发表于《诡丽奇谭》1931 年一月刊。奈亚拉托提普是克苏鲁神话中最重要的神灵之一,是阿撒托斯之子与其信使,执掌混沌、欺骗、阴谋,热衷以不同的化身欺骗并诱惑人类。

And at the last from inner Egypt came

The strange dark One to whom the fellahs bowed;

Silent and lean and cryptically proud,

And wrapped in fabrics red as sunset flame.

Throngs pressed around, frantic for his commands,

But leaving, could not tell what they had heard;

While through the nations spread the awestruck word

That wild beasts followed him and licked his hands.

Soon from the sea a noxious birth began;

Forgotten lands with weedy spires of gold;

The ground was cleft, and mad auroras rolled

Down on the quaking citadels of man.

Then, crushing what he chanced to mould in play,

The idiot Chaos blew Earth's dust away.

而最后从埃及的内陆所前来的
陌生的黑肤者令农夫们纷纷折腰；
沉默、瘦削并带有神秘的倨傲，
身披落日的光焰般火红的衣帛。
人群簇拥而至，为他的命令疯狂，
但离去时却无法说清他们的所闻；
而诸国之中流传着惊叹的言论
据说野兽追随着去舔舐他的手掌。

不久海面下迎来了初生的灾害；
遗忘之地的黄金尖塔上杂草丛生；
大地被撕裂，疯狂的极光翻动
下落在人类岌岌可危的城塞。
然后，当祂把游戏中偶然的造物摧毁，
痴愚混沌之神吹散了地球的飞灰。

阿撒托斯
Azathoth

发表于《诡丽奇谭》1931 年一月刊。阿撒托斯是克苏鲁神话中的主神。

Out in the mindless void the daemon bore me,

Past the bright clusters of dimensioned space,

Till neither time nor matter stretched before me,

But only Chaos, without form or place.

Here the vast Lord of All in darkness muttered

Things he had dreamed but could not understand,

While near him shapeless bat-things flopped and fluttered

In idiot vortices that ray-streams fanned.

They danced insanely to the high, thin whining

Of a cracked flute clutched in a monstrous paw [1],

Whence flow the aimless waves whose chance combining

Gives each frail cosmos its eternal law.

"I am His Messenger," the daemon said,

As in contempt he struck his Master's head.

---

1. a cracked flute clutched in a monstrous paw: 指克苏鲁
神话中的音乐之神特鲁宁布拉。

恶魔在蒙昧的虚空之中将我运载，
穿过标注的空间构成的璀璨星团，
直到时间和物质不复在前方展开，
只剩下混沌，没有形态或地点。
巨大的万物之主在这片黑暗中嘀咕
那些它所梦见却无法理解的事由，
一旁蝙蝠般的无形之物下落并飞舞
直入射线束所激发的痴愚的涡流。

使它们疯狂舞动的高亢尖锐的哀鸣
来自一只可怖的爪子中紧握的长笛，
由此发出的无绪波动间偶然的交融
赋予了每个脆弱的宇宙永恒的定律。
"我是它的信使，"恶魔如是说，
并轻蔑地敲打了自己主人的脑壳。

幻境
Mirage

发表于《诡丽奇谭》1931 年二、三月合刊。作曲家哈罗德·S. 法尔内塞专门为此诗和《上古的信标》谱写了两首同名乐曲。

I do not know if ever it existed—
That lost world floating dimly on Time's stream—
And yet I see it often, violet-misted,
And shimmering at the back of some vague dream.
There were strange towers and curious lapping rivers,
Labyrinths of wonder, and low vaults of light,
And bough-crossed skies of flame, like that which quivers
Wistfully just before a winter's night.

Great moors led off to sedgy shores unpeopled,
Where vast birds wheeled, while on a windswept hill
There was a village, ancient and white-steepled,
With evening chimes for which I listen still.
I do not know what land it is—or dare
Ask when or why I was, or will be, there.

我不知道是否真的曾经存在——
失落的世界暗淡地漂过时间之河——
但我经常见到它，被紫雾所遮盖，
在某些模糊梦境的背面不断闪烁。
那里有陌生之塔和谜样拍动的河流，
奇妙的迷阵，和低矮的光明穹顶，
以及枝干交叉的火红天幕，如同颤抖
当中怀有留恋的冬夜前那片天空。

广袤的荒野通往无人的莎草河岸，
巨鸟们盘旋在此，而狂风吹过的山上
有一座村落，古老并有着白塔高悬，
我在此静静聆听夜晚钟声的鸣响。
我不知道这是哪片土地——也不敢于
询问何时何故我曾在，或将要去，那里。

运河
The Canal

发表于《飘风》1932 年三月刊。

Somewhere in dream there is an evil place
Where tall, deserted buildings crowd along
A deep, black, narrow channel, reeking strong
Of frightful things whence oily currents race.
Lanes with old walls half meeting overhead
Wind off to streets one may or may not know,
And feeble moonlight sheds a spectral glow
Over long rows of windows, dark and dead.

There are no footfalls, and the one soft sound
Is of the oily water as it glides
Under stone bridges, and along the sides
Of its deep flume, to some vague ocean bound.
None lives to tell when that stream washed away
Its dream-lost region from the world of clay.

梦中的某处有一个邪恶的地方
那里高耸的荒弃建筑层层围起
黑暗深邃的狭窄水道，散发着臭气的
可怖之物使油污的浊水流淌。
小巷旁的老墙几乎在头顶交织
延伸至人们或会或不会知悉的街道，
虚弱的月光将幽灵般的光芒照耀
在长列的窗户上面，阴暗又垂死。

那里没有跫音，仅有的轻微响动
只有那油污的浊水正奔流而过
石质桥梁的下方，它顺流远涉
自己深邃的沟渠，模糊地望海而行。
没有生灵知道那条河何时冲刷瓦解
迷失于梦的流域脱离了黏土的世界。

圣蟾寺

St. Toad's

在结集出版前未独立发表。圣蟾这个名字的灵感来自马萨诸塞州马布尔黑德镇青蛙街上的圣米迦勒主教教堂，日后成为克苏鲁神话中蟾蜍之神撒托古亚的别称。

"Beware St. Toad's cracked chimes!" I heard him scream
As I plunged into those mad lanes that wind
In labyrinths obscure and undefined
South of the river where old centuries dream.
He was a furtive figure, bent and ragged,
And in a flash had staggered out of sight,
So still I burrowed onward in the night
Toward where more roof-lines rose, malign and jagged.

No guide-book told of what was lurking here—
But now I heard another old man shriek:
"Beware St. Toad's cracked chimes!" And growing weak,
I paused, when a third greybeard croaked in fear:
"Beware St. Toad's cracked chimes!" Aghast, I fled—
Till suddenly that black spire loomed ahead.

"当心圣蟾寺的疯狂钟声！"我听到他呼喊
同时走进那些狂乱的小巷，它们弯曲
而成的迷宫难以理解又无法定义
位于沉睡着古老纪元的河流南岸。
那是个鬼祟的人影，驼背又衣衫不整，
并在转眼间蹒跚到了我视线外侧，
于是我仍然在黑夜之中不断探索
前路成群升起的屋脊，邪恶又凹凸不平。

没有旅行指南说明此处潜藏着何物——
但此时我听到了另一位老人的惊叫：
"当心圣蟾寺的疯狂钟声！"逐渐缥缈，
我停下，当第三位老者恐惧地发出低呼：
"当心圣蟾寺的疯狂钟声！"我夺命狂奔——
直到黑色的尖塔忽而在面前赫然现身。

魔仆
The Familiars

发表于《飘风》1930 年七月刊。

John Whateley [1] lived about a mile from town,

Up where the hills begin to huddle thick;

We never thought his wits were very quick,

Seeing the way he let his farm run down.

He used to waste his time on some queer books

He'd found around the attic of his place,

Till funny lines got creased into his face,

And folks all said they didn't like his looks.

When he began those night-howls we declared

He'd better be locked up away from harm,

So three men from the Aylesbury town farm

Went for him—but came back alone and scared.

They'd found him talking to two crouching things

That at their step flew off on great black wings.

---

1. Whateley: 惠特利，这个姓氏属于敦威治小镇中召唤外神犹格 - 索托斯的堕落家族。

约翰·惠特利住在镇子的一英里外，

那里的下方开始有山丘层层叠叠；

我们从未想过他事实上才智敏捷，

当看到他把自己的农场经营破败。

他曾经把时间花在某些奇书之中

它们来自他家阁楼里的某个地方，

直到奇怪的纹路弄皱了他的脸庞，

而人们全都声称不喜欢他的面容。

当他开始在夜晚咆哮时我们宣布

他应该被牢牢锁住以免造成祸患，

于是三个人从艾尔斯伯里镇的农田

前去找他——但回来时落单又满脸恐怖。

他们发现与他交谈的两个蜷伏的东西

在他们走近时用巨大的黑翼飞了出去。

上古的信标
The Elder Pharos

发表于《诡丽奇谭》1931 年二、三月合刊。诗中的上
古者被猜测是旧日支配者哈斯塔的化身之一。

From Leng[1], where rocky peaks climb bleak and bare

Under cold stars obscure to human sight,

There shoots at dusk a single beam of light

Whose far blue rays make shepherds whine in prayer.

They say (though none has been there) that it comes

Out of a pharos in a tower of stone,

Where the last Elder One lives on alone,

Talking to Chaos with the beat of drums.

The Thing, they whisper, wears a silken mask

Of yellow, whose queer folds appear to hide

A face not of this earth, though none dares ask

Just what those features are, which bulge inside.

Many, in man's first youth, sought out that glow,

But what they found, no one will ever know.

---

1. Leng: 冷原，克苏鲁神话中的虚构地点，跨越人间与幻梦境的寒冷高原地带，上面生活着多种神话生物。

在冷原，岩石峰荒凉暗淡地升起
在人眼难以辨认的寒冷群星下方，
在黄昏之时这里会投下一束光芒
它渺远的蓝辉使牧羊人祈祷着悲泣。
他们（虽然无人亲临）说那是从
一座石质高塔内的信标灯里射出，
最后的上古者在那里孤独地居住，
与混沌交谈，伴随着鼓点声声。

他们低声说那家伙佩戴的丝绸面巾
颜色橙黄，怪异的褶皱似乎掩藏着
一张不属于地球的脸孔，但无人敢问
肿胀在它下方的面目究竟会是什么。
许多人，在年轻之时，将那处光源寻找，
但他们有何发现，没有人能够知道。

期望
Expectancy

在结集出版前未独立发表。

I cannot tell why some things hold for me

A sense of unplumbed marvels to befall,

Or of a rift in the horizon's wall

Opening to worlds where only gods can be.

There is a breathless, vague expectancy,

As of vast ancient pomps I half recall,

Or wild adventures, uncorporeal,

Ecstasy-fraught, and as a day-dream free.

It is in sunsets and strange city spires,

Old villages and woods and misty downs,

South winds, the sea, low hills, and lighted towns,

Old gardens, half-heard songs, and the moon's fires.

But though its lure alone makes life worth living,

None gains or guesses what it hints at giving.

我无法解释为何有些事对我来讲

意味着深不可测的奇迹即将发生，

或如同地平线幕墙上的一道裂缝

将只有神灵能够存在的世界开放。

那是一种令人屏息，暧昧不明的期望，

源自我模糊记忆中宏伟的古代盛景，

或是恣情的冒险，无影又无形，

满载着狂喜，就像白日中自由的幻想。

它存在于落日和陌生城市的塔尖，

古老的村庄，树林和雾气弥漫的山地，

南风，海洋，矮丘，夜明的城邑，

旧日的花园，朦胧的歌曲，还有月的光焰。

虽则它自身的诱惑使生命具有价值，

无人知悉或猜到它想要给予的暗示。

乡愁
Nostalgia

发表于 1930 年 3 月 12 日的《普罗维登斯日报》。

Once every year, in autumn's wistful glow,
The birds fly out over an ocean waste,
Calling and chattering in a joyous haste
To reach some land their inner memories know.
Great terraced gardens where bright blossoms blow,
And lines of mangoes luscious to the taste,
And temple-groves with branches interlaced
Over cool paths—all these their vague dreams shew.

They search the sea for marks of their old shore—
For the tall city, white and turreted—
But only empty waters stretch ahead,
So that at last they turn away once more.
Yet sunken deep where alien polyps throng,
The old towers miss their lost, remembered song.

乡愁

每年一度，在秋日依依不舍的光热间，
鸟儿们展翅出发将荒芜的海洋越过，
嘤鸣着呼朋唤友，带着欢快的急迫
赶赴它们记忆的深处熟知的地面。
宏伟的阶梯花园有百花争奇斗艳，
和一排排尝起来甘美无比的芒果，
而神庙的树丛当中有着繁枝交错
在幽径之上——它们将一切模糊地梦见。

它们搜寻着当初海岸的标记找遍大海——
搜寻着纯白而布满塔楼的高耸城镇——
但面前只有空荡的海水一望无垠，
所以到最后它们再一次转身离开。
但在异形水螅群聚的沉没深渊之中，
古老的塔怀念着它们消逝的难忘歌声。

背景
Background

发表于 1930 年 4 月 16 日的《普罗维登斯日报》。这首诗的前八行被铭刻在了普罗维登斯布朗大学的约翰·海伊图书馆花园里的洛夫克拉夫特纪念牌匾上。

I never can be tied to raw, new things,
For I first saw the light in an old town,
Where from my window huddled roofs sloped down
To a quaint harbour rich with visionings.
Streets with carved doorways where the sunset beams
Flooded old fanlights and small window-panes,
And Georgian steeples topped with gilded vanes—
These were the sights that shaped my childhood dreams.

Such treasures, left from times of cautious leaven,
Cannot but loose the hold of flimsier wraiths
That flit with shifting ways and muddled faiths
Across the changeless walls of earth and heaven.
They cut the moment's thongs and leave me free
To stand alone before eternity.

初生的新奇事物不会令我留恋，
因为古老的城中我看到最初的灵光，
那里在我窗外，屋脊簇拥着沉降
直到一处视野开阔的古朴港湾。
密布雕花门廊的街头上落日余照
淹没了古老的扇形窗和小小窗格，
乔治亚尖顶的风向标也被镀上金色——
这些景象曾将我儿时的梦境塑造。

这些瑰宝，从谨慎发酵的时光里脱节，
被迫解放了禁锢中气若游丝的幽影，
它们以形态万千和纷乱的信念飞行
将天地构成的亘古不变的墙壁穿越。
它们割断了时刻间的纽带，留下我任意
在永恒前孤单地遗世独立。

居民
The Dweller

发表于 1930 年 5 月 7 日的《普罗维登斯日报》。

It had been old when Babylon was new;
None knows how long it slept beneath that mound,
Where in the end our questing shovels found
Its granite blocks and brought it back to view.
There were vast pavements and foundation-walls,
And crumbling slabs and statues, carved to shew
Fantastic beings of some long ago
Past anything the world of man recalls.

And then we saw those stone steps leading down
Through a choked gate of graven dolomite
To some black haven of eternal night
Where elder signs and primal secrets frown.
We cleared a path—but raced in mad retreat
When from below we heard those clumping feet.

当巴比伦初建之时它已经垂垂年迈；

无人知晓它在土堆下沉睡了多长时间，

直到最后我们的勘探铲在那里发现

它花岗岩的砖石才使得它重现光彩。

那里有着巨大的人行道和基础墙体，

以及破碎的石板和塑像，被雕刻而成

某种年代久远的不可思议的生灵

超出了人世间能够记起的任何东西。

随后我们看到那些石阶向下延伸

穿过一扇雕花的大理石门的阻塞

直至某个永夜当中的庇护之所

旧神之印与原始的秘密在此眉头皱紧。

我们清理出通道——却逃窜得慌不择路

当听到那些沉重的脚步从下方传出。

异化
Alienation

发表于《诡丽奇谭》1931 年四、五月合刊。本诗的情节近似于对小说《雾中怪屋》的改写。

His solid flesh had never been away,

For each dawn found him in his usual place,

But every night his spirit loved to race

Through gulfs and worlds remote from common day.

He had seen Yaddith [1], yet retained his mind,

And come back safely from the Ghooric zone [2],

When one still night across curved space was thrown

That beckoning piping from the voids behind.

He waked that morning as an older man,

And nothing since has looked the same to him.

Objects around float nebulous and dim—

False, phantom trifles of some vaster plan.

His folk and friends are now an alien throng

To which he struggles vainly to belong.

---

1. Yaddith: 亚狄斯，克苏鲁神话中的虚构行星，上面的文明已被巨噬蠕虫摧毁。

2. Ghooric zone: 古里科地带，黑暗行星犹格斯附近的小行星带。

他真实可触的肉体从未不辞而别，

每个黎明都能发现他在同一地方，

但每个夜里他的灵魂欣然地飞扬

穿过远离平凡时光的深渊与诸界。

他曾见到亚狄斯，却仍然保有理性，

并从古里科地带安然无恙地归返，

当跨越扭曲空间的静谧之夜充满

从身后虚空中传来的诱惑笛声。

他在那个清晨醒来后变得老去，

自此眼中的一切都已不复当初。

万物在身边昏暗模糊地飘浮——

作为某张庞大绘图错谬的零光片羽。

如今他的家人和朋友是群外星居民

而他徒劳地尝试着想要融入他们。

海港笛声
Harbour Whistles

发表于《银蕨》1930 年五月刊。

Over old roofs and past decaying spires
The harbour whistles chant all through the night;
Throats from strange ports, and beaches far and white,
And fabulous oceans, ranged in motley choirs.
Each to the other alien and unknown,
Yet all, by some obscurely focussed force
From brooding gulfs beyond the Zodiac's course,
Fused into one mysterious cosmic drone.

Through shadowy dreams they send a marching line
Of still more shadowy shapes and hints and views;
Echoes from outer voids, and subtle clues
To things which they themselves cannot define.
And always in that chorus, faintly blent,
We catch some notes no earth-ship ever sent.

飞越古老的屋顶和衰朽的塔楼

海港的笛声吟唱着响彻夜晚；

低鸣发自异港，和白色的远滩，

连同壮美的海洋汇成凌乱的合奏。

它们彼此之间陌生而无法相认，

但由于某种力量无形间的集聚，

自黄道轨迹下幽冥的峡湾发起，

被融入同一曲神秘的宇宙杂音。

在昏暗的梦里它们派来的远征队列

包含有影影绰绰的轮廓、预兆和景致；

回响自外层的虚空，那微妙的暗示

所指的事情它们自身亦不能明确。

而那曲合唱之中，总是隐约地混入，

我们耳边并非来自地球船只的音符。

重拾
Recapture

发表于《诡丽奇谭》1930 年五月刊。R. H. 巴洛曾认为此诗适合作为组诗的收尾之作，但洛夫克拉夫特坚持将其放在这个位置："我想《重拾》最好作为组诗的第三十四篇——而《黄昏之星》和《连续性》分别是三十五篇和三十六篇。《重拾》似乎在气质上相比另外两首更加专注并且局限，因而最好放在它们之前——使得真菌们能够走向带有更多发散性思维的结尾。"

The way led down a dark, half-wooded heath

Where moss-grey boulders humped above the mould,

And curious drops, disquieting and cold,

Sprayed up from unseen streams in gulfs beneath.

There was no wind, nor any trace of sound

In puzzling shrub, or alien-featured tree,

Nor any view before—till suddenly,

Straight in my path, I saw a monstrous mound.

Half to the sky those steep sides loomed upspread,

Rank-grassed, and cluttered by a crumbling flight

Of lava stairs that scaled the fear-topped height

In steps too vast for any human tread.

I shrieked—and knew what primal star and year

Had sucked me back from man's dream-transient sphere!

这条路通往树木稀疏的暗色荒原

那里生苔的巨石隆起在腐土之上，

离奇古怪的水滴，带着慑人的冰凉，

由下界深渊中的无形之溪向外喷溅。

此地无风，也没有一丝声音会从

迷乱的灌木或奇形怪状的树上响起，

视野中空无一物——直到突然之际，

我看到道路前方一座骇人的山垄。

陡峭的斜坡赫然向半空中伸出，

绿草成排，并且布满了坍塌的一列

顶部升入了可怖高度的熔岩台阶

那些巨大的梯级并不适合凡人立足。

我尖叫——并明白是怎样原始的星辰和年代

将我从人类梦幻泡影般的畛域中吸了回来！

黄昏之星
Evening Star

发表于《先驱》1932 年秋季刊。

I saw it from that hidden, silent place
Where the old wood half shuts the meadow in.
It shone through all the sunset's glories—thin
At first, but with a slowly brightening face.
Night came, and that lone beacon, amber-hued,
Beat on my sight as never it did of old;
The evening star—but grown a thousandfold
More haunting in this hush and solitude.

It traced strange pictures on the quivering air—
Half-memories that had always filled my eyes—
Vast towers and gardens; curious seas and skies
Of some dim life—I never could tell where.
But now I knew that through the cosmic dome
Those rays were calling from my far, lost home.

我在隐秘的寂静之地将它观望
那里古老的树林几乎将草地合围
它的光芒穿过落日余照——隐微
在先，但面容渐渐地变得明亮。
夜幕降临，那琥珀色的孤独信标
前所未有地在我视线当中闪烁；
那是黄昏之星——却变得千倍的
摄人心魂，由于这沉默与寂寥。

它在空气颤动中描绘出诡异的图谱——
那些朦胧的记忆总是充斥我的眼睛——
巨大的塔与花园；奇异的海洋与天空
来自昏暗的浮生——我不知道那是何处。
但此刻我明白穿越过宇宙的穹面
那些光芒自我遥远的失落家园呼唤。

连续性
Continuity

发表于《先驱》1932 年夏季刊。

There is in certain ancient things a trace
Of some dim essence—more than form or weight;
A tenuous aether, indeterminate,
Yet linked with all the laws of time and space.
A faint, veiled sign of continuities
That outward eyes can never quite descry;
Of locked dimensions harbouring years gone by,
And out of reach except for hidden keys.

It moves me most when slanting sunbeams glow
On old farm buildings set against a hill,
And paint with life the shapes which linger still
From centuries less a dream than this we know.
In that strange light I feel I am not far
From the fixt mass whose sides the ages are.

在特定的古老事物中有一丝痕迹
显现隐约的特质——超出形态或质量；
那是种纤柔的以太，变化无常，
却连接着时间与空间所有的定律。
那微弱、含蓄的预兆中的连续性
令浮于表面的眼眸无法真正发觉；
它锁起的维度蕴含着流逝的岁月，
除隐藏的钥匙之外无计可以触碰。

它最令我触动是当倾泻的阳光照耀
在依山而建的古老农场建筑上面，
用生命绘制而成萦绕不去的图案
缘起的世纪不似我们如梦的今朝。
在奇异的光中我感觉自己已经贴近
由时代的层面汇聚而成的牢固集群。

Bouts Rimés

和韵诗

创作于 1934 年 5 月。和韵诗是一种源自法国的
文字游戏，由出题者提前拟好诗歌的尾韵，再交给诗
人完成全诗。本诗的尾韵由 R. H. 巴洛拟定。

津巴布韦外
Beyond Zimbabwe

The drums of the jungle in ecstasy boom,
And summon the chosen to torture and doom;
The quivering throngs wait expectant and sad,
While the shrieks of the priest echo drunkenly mad.
Round the altars are tributes of barley and cream,
And the acolytes stagger in opiate dream.
It is thus that the Shadow grows mighty and whole,
As it feeds on the body and sucks at the soul.

密林中的鼓声正狂热地敲响，
召唤选民们散布劫难与灭亡。
颤抖的人群悲哀迫切地等待，
祭司回荡的高呼迷醉而病态。
大麦与奶油的贡品摆满祭坛，
侍僧们在麻醉剂之梦中蹒跚。
就这样暗影变得强烈且完整，
饱餐着肉体并且吸干了心灵。

白象
The White Elephant

Dim in the past from primal chaos rose

That form with mottled cloak and scaly hose

Who bade the lesser ghouls to earn their bread,

Perform dread rites, and echo what he said.

They bred the leprous tree and poison flower

And pressed dim aeons into one black hour.

Wherefore we pray, as pious pagans must,

To the white beast he shaped from fungous dust.

遥远的过去当原初的混沌升起
斑驳斗篷之下长鼻覆鳞的神祇
吩咐低阶的食尸鬼们自寻生路，
举行可怖的仪式将它所言复述。
它们种下麻风之树和剧毒花朵
将阴晦的万古凝于至暗的一刻。
作为虔信之徒，我们必须祈求，
它用真菌粉尘塑造的白色巨兽。

在爱伦·坡曾经踏足的一处僻静的普罗维登斯教堂墓地
In a Sequester'd Providence Churchyard Where Once Poe Walk'd

创作于 1936 年 8 月，当时诗人与诗友 R. H. 巴洛、阿道夫·德·卡斯特罗一同参访了普罗维登斯的圣约翰教堂墓地，每个人都为纪念在 1848—1849 年到访此地的爱伦·坡创作了一首诗歌。

Eternal brood [1] *the shadows on this ground,*
Dreaming of centuries that have gone before;
Great elms rise solemnly by slab and mound,
Arch'd high above a hidden world of yore.
Round all the scene a light of memory plays,
And dead leaves whisper of departed days,
Longing for sights and sounds that are no more.

Lonely and sad, a spectre glides along
Aisles where of old his living footsteps fell;
No common glance discerns him, tho' his song
Peals down thro' time with a mysterious spell:
Only the few who sorcery's secret know
Espy amidst these tombs the shade of Poe.

---

1. Eternal brood: 化用自斯宾塞《仙后》中的诗句 "th'eternal brood of glorie excellent"。

在爱伦·坡曾经踏足的一处僻静的普罗维登斯教堂墓地。

不朽的子嗣在此地化为阴影，
梦想着久已逝去的百年时光；
参天榆树在石板与土丘旁上升，
将往昔的隐秘世界遮在下方。
一束回忆之光在此景四周摇曳，
枯死的叶片在轻诉消逝的岁月，
渴望着不复存在的景象与声响。

孤寂又悲戚，一个幽灵悄然飘过
往日他鲜活的脚步曾踏过的小道；
没有肉眼将他认出，虽然他的歌
和神秘的咒语仍在一同余音萦绕：
只有少数人得以知晓巫术的秘密
在这些坟墓之间看到了坡的影迹。

致芬利先生，关于他为布洛克先生的故事《无面之神》所作之画

To Mr. Finlay, upon His Drawing for Mr. Bloch's Tale, "The Faceless God"

发表于《幻影成像》1937年五月刊。这首诗本是洛夫克拉夫特在私人信件中写给维吉尔·芬利的一首赠诗。《无面之神》是发表于《诡丽奇谭》1936年五月刊的一篇小说，芬利先生为其创作的插画堪称杂志有史以来最好的插画之一。

In dim abysses pulse the shapes of night,
　　Hungry and hideous, with strange mitres crown'd;
Black pinions beating in fantastic flight
　　From orb to orb thro' sunless void profound.
None dares to name the cosmos whence they course,
　　Or guess the look on each amorphous face,
Or speak the words that with resistless force
　　Would draw them from the hells of outer space.

Yet here upon a page our frighten'd glance
　　Finds monstrous forms no human eye should see;
Hints of those blasphemies whose countenance
　　Spreads death and madness thro' infinity.
What limner he who braves black gulfs alone
　　And lives to make their alien horrors known?

428

致芬利先生，关于他为布洛克先生的故事《无面之神》所作之画。

那座幽暗的渊谷充满黑夜的影像，

　　饥渴又丑恶，头戴有诡异的冠冕；

在怪诞的飞翔中拍动的漆黑翅膀

　　游走于星体穿越无光虚空的深渊。

无人敢于说出它们来自哪片寰宇，

　　或猜测每张无形的面庞上的神色，

或说出那些力量不可违抗的咒语

　　使得它们从外层空间的地狱解脱。

但在这纸页之上我们惊恐的瞻顾

　　发现了人眼不应看到的可怖身影；

暗示当中那些僭妄亵渎的面目

　　将死亡与疯狂传播直至于永恒。

怎样的一位画家敢将漆黑的鸿沟面对

　　并且活着将这些异星的恐怖描绘？

429

致克拉克·阿什顿·史密斯
先生，关于他想象奇绝的故
事、诗歌、画作以及雕塑
To Clark Ashton Smith, Esq.,
upon His Phantastick Tales,
Verses, Pictures, and Sculptures

发表于《诡丽奇谭》1938年四月刊。这首诗曾经被诗
人在很多信件中引用。克拉克·阿什顿·史密斯（1893—
1961），美国作家，洛夫克拉夫特的密友，克苏鲁神话的奠
基人之一。

A time-black tower against dim banks of cloud;

   Around its base the pathless, pressing wood.

Shadow and silence, moss and mould, enshroud

   Grey, age-fell'd slabs that once as cromlechs stood.

No fall of foot, no song of bird awakes

   The lethal aisles of sempiternal night,

Tho' oft with stir of wings the dense air shakes,

   As in the tower there glows a pallid light.

For here, apart, dwells one whose hands have wrought

   Strange eidola that chill the world with fear;

Whose graven runes in tones of dread have taught

   What things beyond the star-gulfs lurk and leer.

Dark Lord of Averoigne [1]*—whose windows stare*

   On pits of dream no other gaze could bear!

---

1. Averoigne: 亚威隆尼，史密斯虚构的中世纪法国地名，神话生物和恐怖事件频频在此出现。

致克拉克·阿什顿·史密斯先生，关于他想象奇绝的故事、诗歌、画作以及雕塑。

一座古旧的高塔伸向朦胧的云河之堤；

　　在它的基座旁是无人涉足的繁密树林。

阴影与死寂，青苔与霉菌，一同遮蔽

　　曾屹立于石阵却被岁月伐倒的灰暗石墩。

没有脚步落下，也没有鸟的歌声唤醒

　　这永恒的夜晚之中致命的诸条甬道，

虽然稠密的空气常随飘摆的羽翼颤动，

　　当一束苍白的光线自塔中向外照耀。

在这里，有位独居者用他的双手造就

　　诡异的幻灵进而为世界带来恐怖；

他以雕刻成可畏的色调的符文讲授

　　在群星的鸿沟下潜伏并睨视的异物。

黑暗的亚威隆尼之主——你的窗口直面

　　他人的凝视所不能承受的梦境深渊！

纳希卡娜
Nathicana

发表于《漂泊者》1927年春季刊。洛夫克拉夫特在给唐纳德·旺德莱的一封信中称此诗为"对毫无实在意义的夸张文体的戏仿",唐纳德·旺德莱则评价此诗为"一种罕有而奇特的文学怪胎,这首讽刺作品出色到超越戏仿而拥有原创性"。除扎伊斯和阿施塔特外,诗中出现的一切专有名词皆来自叙事者的臆想并仅出现在本诗中。

It was in the pale garden of Zaïs[1];

The mist-shrouded gardens of Zaïs,

Where blossoms the white nephalotë,

The redolent herald of midnight.

There slumber the still lakes of crystal,

And streamlets that flow without murm'ring;

Smooth streamlets from caverns of Kathos

Where brood the calm spirits of twilight.

And over the lakes and the streamlets

Are bridges of pure alabaster,

White bridges all cunningly carven

With figures of fairies and daemons.

Here glimmer strange suns and strange planets,

1.Zaïs: 扎伊斯，法国作曲家、管风琴家、音乐理论家让 - 菲
利普·拉莫（1683—1764）创作的歌剧《扎伊斯》中的主人公。
扎伊斯是空气之精灵，为了赢得牧羊女泽利迪的芳心而幻化为
牧羊人，在历经一系列考验后两人终成眷属。

纳希卡娜

那是在苍白的扎伊斯花园；

氤氲着雾气的扎伊斯花园，

那里绽开的白色拿非利之泪，

用芳香预示着午夜的到来。

那里沉睡着静谧的水晶之湖，

以及悄无声息地流淌的小溪；

平缓的溪水源自凯索的洞穴

宁静的暮光之灵在此处沉思。

而在这些湖泊与溪流之上

有着雪花石膏筑成的桥梁，

洁白的桥身皆被精心雕琢

刻上了仙子与精灵的姿影。

奇异的恒星和星群在此闪耀，

And strange is the crescent Banapis

That sets yond the ivy-grown ramparts

Where thickens the dust of the evening.

Here fall the white vapours of Yabon;

And here in the swirl of vapours

I saw the divine Nathicana;

The garlanded, white Nathicana;

The slender, black-hair'd Nathicana;

The sloe-ey'd, red-lipp'd Nathicana;

The silver-voic'd, sweet Nathicana;

The pale-rob'd, belov'd Nathicana.

And ever was she my belovèd,

From ages when Time was unfashion'd;

From days when the stars were not fashion'd

Nor any thing fashion'd but Yabon.

And here dwelt we ever and ever,

The innocent children of Zaïs,

At peace in the paths and the arbours,

White-crown'd with the blest nephalotë.

How oft would we float in the twilight

O'er flow'r-cover'd pastures and hillsides

而最为奇异的芭纳匹斯之月

升起在爬满青藤的墙壁上方

那里黄昏的烟尘正变得浓郁。

亚波恩白色的水雾在此飘散；

而在这片水雾的涡旋之中

我看到了圣洁的纳希卡娜；

头戴花环，纯白的纳希卡娜；

身材窈窕，黑发的纳希卡娜；

眼眸乌黑，红唇的纳希卡娜；

声如银铃，甜美的纳希卡娜；

白袍加身，挚爱的纳希卡娜，

长久以来我都深爱着伊人，

自从一开始时间尚未定型；

自从一开始星辰尚未形成

除亚波恩外万物尚未诞生。

而我们永生永世栖居在这里，

作为扎伊斯园中纯真的孩子，

置身安宁的小径和凉亭之间，

头戴拿非利之泪的神圣花环。

我们经常在黄昏的时候飘荡

俯瞰鲜花覆盖的牧场与山坡

All white with the lowly astalthon;

The lowly yet lovely astalthon,

And dream in a world made of dreaming

The dreams that are fairer than Aidenn;

Bright dreams that are truer than reason!

So dream'd and so lov'd we thro' ages,

Till came the curs'd season of Dzannin;

The daemon-damn'd season of Dzannin;

When red shone the suns and the planets,

And red gleam'd the crescent Banapis,

And red fell the vapours of Yabon.

Then redden'd the blossoms and streamlets

And lakes that lay under the bridges,

And even the calm alabaster

Glow'd pink with uncanny reflections

Till all the carv'd fairies and daemons

Leerd redly from the backgrounds of shadow.

Now redden'd my vision, and madly

I strove to peer thro' the dense curtain

And glimpse the divine Nathicana;

The pure, ever-pale Nathicana;

纳希卡娜

皎然盛开着卑微的埃斯塔森;

那卑微而又可爱的埃斯塔森,

并在幻想的世界里做着美梦

那些梦境比天堂还要美妙;

明亮的梦真实得超出理智!

我们梦想并痴恋着共度流年,

直到迎来了万恶的赞宁时节;

那被魔鬼所诅咒的赞宁时节;

恒星与星群发出赤色的光辉,

芭纳匹斯之月在殷红中闪耀,

而亚波恩的水雾鲜血般洒落。

于是血色染上了鲜花与溪流

以及在桥梁之下静卧的湖水,

甚至连那肃穆的雪花石膏

都发出异乎寻常的粉色反光

所有精雕细琢的仙子与精灵

在阴影的背景中以红眼睨视。

我的视野一片血红,并狂乱地

试图得以望穿那浓厚的帷幕

再度瞥见神圣的纳希卡娜;

一尘不染,永洁的纳希卡娜;

The lov'd, the unchang'd Nathicana.
But vortex on vortex of madness
Beclouded my labouring vision;
My damnable, reddening vision
That built a new world for my seeing;
A new world of redness and darkness,
A horrible coma call'd living.
So now in this coma call'd living
I view the bright phantons of beauty;
The false, hollow phantoms of beauty
That cloak all the evils of Dzannin.
I view them with infinite longing,
So like do they seem to my lov'd one;
So shapely and fair like my lov'd one;
Yet foul from their eyes shines their evil;
Their cruel and pitiless evil,
More evil than Thaphron and Latgoz,
Twice ill for its gorgeous concealment.
And only in slumbers of midnight
Appears the lost maid Nathicana,
The pallid, the pure Nathicana,

纳希卡娜

我心所爱，不变的纳希卡娜。

但是重重漩涡叠起的疯狂

遮蔽了我疲惫不堪的视线；

我那诅咒之下血红的视线

将一个新的世界树立在眼中；

这个新的世界充满红黑两色，

这段骇人的沉睡被称为人生。

身处于这段实为沉睡的人生

我见到了明艳而美丽的幻觉；

那些虚假空洞而美丽的幻觉

掩藏着来自赞宁的一切罪恶。

我带着无尽的渴求望向她们

她们看起来多像是我的挚爱；

曼妙而美丽得如同我的挚爱；

但她们污秽的眼中透出罪孽；

她们残忍又冷酷无情的罪孽，

更甚于塔弗隆或是莱特戈斯，

有着两倍于迷人外表的恶毒。

而我只有在午夜的沉睡之际

能见到迷失的少女纳希卡娜，

苍白虚弱，纯净的纳希卡娜，

Who fades at the glance of the dreamer.
Again and again do I seek her;
I woo with deep draughts of Plathotis,
Deep draughts brew'd in wine of Astarte
And strengthen'd with tears of long weeping.
I yearn for the gardens of Zaïs;
The lovely lost garden of Zaïs
Where blossoms the white nephalotë,
The redolent herald of midnight.
The last potent draught I am brewing;
A draught that the daemons delight in;
A draught that will banish the redness;
The horrible coma call'd living.
Soon, soon, if I fail not in brewing,
The redness and madness will vanish,
And deep in the worm-peopled darkness
Will rot the base chains that hav' bound me.
Once more shall the gardens of Zaïs
Dawn white on my long-tortur'd vision,
And there midst the vapours of Yabon
Will stand the divine Nathicana;

444

纳希卡娜

被梦中人轻瞥一眼便会消散。

我一次又一次地将伊人追寻；

借助一种柏拉索提斯的药剂

药剂由阿施塔特的美酒酿制

并由于长年的泪水更加浓烈。

我深深渴望着扎伊斯花园；

可爱而失落的扎伊斯花园

那里绽开的白色拿非利之泪，

用芳香预示着午夜的到来。

最后我酿制了这种强力药剂；

这药剂能令精灵们感到欢欣；

这药剂能够消除眼前的血红；

这段骇人的沉睡被称为人生。

快了，快了，若酿制不失败，

血红和疯狂很快会永远消失，

而在蠕虫居住的黑暗深渊之内

禁锢着我的锁链也将彻底腐朽。

扎伊斯花园必定会再度降临

在我饱受折磨的眼中映入曙光，

而在那片亚波恩的水雾之中

将会伫立着神圣的纳希卡娜；

The deathless, restor'd Nathicana

Whose like is not met with in living.

永生不灭，复原的纳希卡娜
如斯存在只能邂逅于人生之外。

图书在版编目(CIP)数据

诗集:来自犹格斯的真菌:汉英对照/(美)H．P．
洛夫克拉夫特(H.P.Lovecraft)著;刘华清译. —— 重
庆:重庆大学出版社,2022.4(2022.8重印)
ISBN 978-7-5689-2997-4

Ⅰ.①诗… Ⅱ.①H… ②刘… Ⅲ.①英语－汉语－
对照读物 ②诗集－美国－现代 Ⅳ.①H319.4:I

中国版本图书馆CIP数据核字(2021)第227764号

诗集:来自犹格斯的真菌:汉英对照

SHIJI: LAIZI YOUGESI DE ZHENJUN: HANYINGDUIZHAO

〔美〕H.P.洛夫克拉夫特 著

刘华清 译

责任编辑:李佳熙

责任校对:王 倩

责任印刷:张 策

装帧设计:□□□DESIGN

插 画:陈 华 珠子酱

重庆大学出版社出版发行

出版人:饶帮华

社址:重庆市沙坪坝区大学城西路21号

电话:(023) 88617190 88617185(中小学)

传真:(023) 88617186 88617166

网址:http://www.cqup.com.cn

全国新华书店经销

印刷:重庆升光电力印务有限公司

开本:787mm×1092mm 1/32 印张:14.25 字数:220千

2022年4月第1版 2022年8月第2次印刷

ISBN 978-7-5689-2997-4 定价:59.00元